A Vertical Leap Seminar is a power-packed boot camp designed to fast track participants through a Vertical Leap from FACTS to FAITH to ACTION! The goal of the seminar is achieved when participants can crystallize their God-given dreams, visions, and ideas and are empowered to pursue them.

The Vertical Leap Seminar teaches how to:

- Take an action and give birth to a dream, vision, or idea from God
- Take godly risks
- Apply kingdom commerce principles to the home, business, church, and community
- Start a godly business
- Apply total quality management systems to ministry, business, and personal life
- Write a business plan, understand business financial statements, and much more

You may attend a four-day Vertical Leap Seminar held at the Alhatti Christian Resort in the mountains above Palm Springs, California, or you may host a Vertical Leap Seminar City Tour in your community. For more information, call: 1-888-559-BOSS or visit the web site at: www.bossthemovement.com

The Vertical Leap seminar cost is $399.99 per person. This price includes accommodations for 4 days and 3 nights at the beautiful Alhatti Christian Resort, 2 meals per day (continental breakfast and full dinner) plus all training material. (Lunch can be purchased at an additional cost of $8.50 per meal.)

Mr.
Mrs. _____

      Name   Title

Address _____

City, State Zip _____

Day phone: _____ Evening phone: _____

Reason for attending Vertical Leap:
Personal / Business / Ministry / B.O.S.S. Trainer (circle one)

Arrival Date and Time

Method of Payment:
Cash / Check / Money Order / Credit Card (circle one)

Payment Type: Deposit / Payment in Full / Payment Plan / (circle one)

Make check or money order payable to: **Alhatti Resort**
P.O. Box 55216
Diamond Bar, CA 91765
For shuttle information and/or early arrival call:
1-888-559-BOSS or 909-861-3846

Office Use Only

❏ Confirmation letter mailed? _____ Date mailed: _____
❏ Contract mailed? (if applies) _____
Accommodations:
❏ Male dorm ❏ Female dorm ❏ Male cottage ❏ Female cottage
❏ Special requirements: _____
❏ Check enclosed payable to: **Alhatti Resort**
❏ Check # _____ Check amount _____
❏ Charge to: ❏ Mastercard ❏ Visa ❏ AmEx ❏ Discover
❏ Card number _____
❏ Expiration date _____
❏ Signature _____

TM

VERTICAL LEAP:
From FACTS to FAITH
to ACTION

Al Hollingsworth
with Deborah Poulalion

VERTICAL LEAP by Al Hollingsworth

Published by:
Insight Publishing Group
8801 South Yale, Suite 410
Tulsa, OK 74137
918-493-1718

Scripture quotations marked KJV are from the King James Version of the Bible.

Scripture quotations marked TLB are from The Living Bible. Copyright © 1971 by Tyndale House Publishers. Used by permission.

Scripture quotations marked NKJV are from the New King James Version of the Bible. Copyright © 1979,1980,1982 by Thomas Nelson Inc., publishers. Used by permission.

International Standard Book Number: 890900-26-5
Library of Congress Card Catalog Number: 99-76084

Dedication

This book is dedicated to all believers in Jesus Christ who feel God's call to be in right alignment with His purpose and desire training in how to birth His dreams, visions, and ideas.

Acknowledgments

First to my Lord and Savior, Jesus Christ, who each day reminds me that He loves me, that He has a plan for me, to be at peace with the challenges of life and to trust Him for He is with me. Thank You for Your love and patience with me.

To my wife and best friend, Hattie, who is always by my side as lover, counselor, visionary, and motivator, who is ever ready to leave the comforts of home to be with me as we travel and discover the truths of this world. Thank you for the years of challenging me to write a life-changing, interactive book.

To my children and grandchildren, who have taught me love and patience in the issues of life's success.

To my anointed co-laborer in the delivery of this book, Debbie Poulalion, thank you for your faithfulness, persistence, and hard work in the midst of pregnancy and delivery while yet managing with husband, Mark, a beautiful family.

To Dr. Myles Munroe, thank you for being a man of vision who has touched the world with hope and purpose. Continue to roar—we are awake and listening. Your advice and encouragement have been most appreciated.

To my Aldelano, CBM (Christian Business Ministries), and Alhatti teams—past and present—who have helped me to reach my dreams, visions, and ideas.

CONTENTS

Diagrams and Illustrations

Foreword
by Dr. Myles Munroe

The desire to achieve and succeed is inherent in the heart of all humans no matter their socio-economic status. However, only a small percentage of the world's population will experience the level of success desired.

This lack of personal achievement is due in some cases to lack of opportunity, disadvantaged situations, and external resources restrictions. However, in the majority of the cases, many fail to achieve their God-given purpose and potential due to their ignorance of, or failure to effectively apply, the eternal principles and laws of life established by the Creator.

Life was designed for success and created for you and I to achieve and experience God's destiny and vision for our lives. However, life was also designed to function according to set laws and principles that guarantee success. If we can learn and apply these laws as laid down by the Creator of life, success would be inevitable.

Al Hollingsworth in this work, *Vertical Leap,* breaks down these fundamental principles for all of us to apply and, through his personal experience and achievements, makes them simple and practical. In his direct approach, Al leaps over complicated formulas and theories to present these vital principles from the source of all wisdom, the Bible.

Vertical Leap shows us that no matter where we are, in what situation we may find ourselves, or our economic condition, if we follow these time-tested laws of success, we can make that Vertical Leap to the place of success designed for each of us by our Creator God.

Al's personal testimony and living example is evidence that what he writes is proven and true. I admonish you to carefully peel the wisdom and insight from these pages and, through diligent application and commitment, watch your life also make that Vertical Leap.

—DR. MYLES MUNROE
Nassau, Bahamas

VERTICAL LEAP™

Part I

How to Get
What You Want

Chapter I

Stop Being Sorry

Many of us have good intentions about our dreams, but we frequently find ourselves following up those intentions with the words, "I'm sorry." I'm sorry I didn't complete it; I'm sorry it didn't happen. I'm sorry, I'm sorry, I'm so sorry.

We say I'm sorry so much that it has shaped our perception of ourselves—we *are* sorry.

We've seen so much failure around us that we think success is out of our reach. We look at others who succeed and think, "They must have a golden spoon or something I'm not privy to. I am just destined to be sorry." We find a sick form of contentment in believing we were predestined for failure.

Guess what? Success is out of reach unless you

believe that you can have it. Unless you believe, you won't take action. And if you don't take action, you will never succeed.

I have written *Vertical Leap* to tell you that God wants you to succeed. In fact, He purposed for you to succeed because He placed dreams, visions and ideas inside of you that are crucial to fulfilling His purposes on earth. Success isn't just about your personal happiness. It's about God's plan for humanity.

Vertical Leap is not a book about self-motivation. It's a book about finding out what God has for you to do, building up your faith and taking action.

A lot of people call me Coach because of the way I challenge and encourage people around me. For the rest of this book I want to be your one-on-one trainer. Together we can break the "I'm-sorry" cycle.

Reading a book may be a challenge for you, but I guarantee that if you apply yourself and do it that you will be amazed at the benefits you will reap.

As your personal trainer, I have a plan that will make taking the Vertical Leap easy and efficient. Just as when you are working out, don't get bogged down by trying to do it all at once. Short, ongoing reading sessions will make you stronger than exhausting yourself and then doing nothing for a month.

Here's your personalized workout plan.

Key Concepts Reading Plan

Let's make reading this book easy. Below is a list of key concepts and the page numbers that explain them. If you read just one key concept per day, you will finish the entire book in thirty-three days!

Chapter 1 "Stop Being Sorry"

- ❏ Day 1: Satan's strategies (pp. 6–11)
- ❏ Day 2: Motivation (pp. 11–14)
- ❏ Day 3: Application questions (pp. 14–15)

Chapter 2 "Vertical Leap"

- ❏ Day 4: Stay conscious/Do it now (pp. 16–19)
- ❏ Day 5: Your potential (pp. 19–26)
- ❏ Day 6: Application questions (pp. 26–27)

Chapter 3 "See It on the Inside"

- ❏ Day 7: Faith vs. Logic (pp. 3o–35)
- ❏ Day 8: Parallel universes (pp. 35–38)
- ❏ Day 9: Application questions (pp. 38–39)

Chapter 4 "Bond With Your Source"

- ❏ Day 10: Levels of bonding (pp. 40–47)
- ❏ Day 11: Heroes of faith (pp. 47–52)
- ❏ Day 12: Application questions (p. 53)

Chapter 5 "Make the Invisible Visible"

- ❏ Day 13: Hope to a Thing (pp. 54–60)
- ❏ Day 14: Mark 11:22-25 formula (pp. 60–62)
- ❏ Day 15: Rules of operation in the spirit realm (pp. 63–69)
- ❏ Day 16: Application questions (pp. 69–70)

Chapter 6 "Create; Don't Just Trade"

Chapter 7 "Reprogram Your Subconscious Mind"

Chapter 8 "Choose Who Pushes You"

Chapter 9 "Analyze Your System"

Chapter 10 "Seeking Spiritual Guidance"

If you are willing to be obedient and try, God will give you another chance to bring forth your visions and dreams—or He will give you better ones. I know this from personal experience.

My Second Chance

Early in my business career I was not having financial success. This condition continued for many years until one day my wife, Hattie, and I asked God to remove anything in our lives that was not pleasing to Him. Shortly afterward, He answered that prayer—Hattie and I went bankrupt.

I thought that was the worst thing that ever happened to me. How could God allow this? That prayer was not intended to include removing my business, my livelihood, my love! The business had been good for my pride. I had big impressive buildings, machines, and trucks on the road carrying my logo.

After seventeen years of running a multimillion-dollar business, it was gone in one swoop. Creditors foreclosed and shut me down. This was a dark time of my soul. I was so confused. I thought I had things all together. Now I was losing all the things on which I had built my identity.

For nine months, my suffering drove me into the hills near my home, crying out for hours each day for God's clarity and direction in my life, "God, I'm going to find You or die. I'm not going to play church with You anymore. I'm not going to play games and say I understand things about You when I can't see. God, I need You to be present with me. Give me a new dream, a vision, or an idea."

Out of that desperate cry was birthed our multi-million-dollar contract packaging business

(Aldelano Corporation). That successful business has provided enough income for us to launch several ministries:

- B.O.S.S. the Movement (aimed at training inner-city teens for business),
- Christian Business Ministries (teaching business principles to adults),
- The Alhatti Christian Resort (located near Palm Springs, California), and
- Vertical Leap Seminars (see page i for information on how to attend).

Now I thank God for this time of learning to trust Him. The wilderness experience allowed God to give us a new vision for business so profitable that we could be a blessing in building the kingdom of God and retire if we chose to without ever having to be financially sorry. I am filled with excitement as I travel and work every day because I know that I am fulfilling God's dream for me, which in turn benefits all of humanity as my dream fits into His greater plans.

Satan's Strategies

Satan doesn't want us to give birth to the vision God places in us. He uses five simple strategies to paralyze us.

1. Fear. We're afraid that if we try, we will fail. But the Word of God says, "Fear not, for I am with thee" (Gen. 26:24, KJV). Fearful thinking will birth a spirit of indecisiveness and powerlessness. The greatest threat to faith is the fear of failing.

2. Weariness. We get into bad habits because

7

we're tired. I am frequently asked to conduct marriage seminars. When I first started studying why marriages aren't working, I thought the reasons would be money and then sex. But the number one problem was "I'm tired." Weariness can birth a spirit of laziness, which manifests as uncleanness and crystallizes into poverty and selfish dependence.

All day you worry and fret about the cares of the world. "I may be laid off tomorrow. I may not be able to pay the car note and put food on the table. I don't know if they like me here; they might reject me there." Weariness is one way Satan keeps the body of Christ from hearing God.

3. Lack of Discipline. What's your grade point average in life? Are you flunking and repeating the same class over and over again? If so, you are probably choosing to satisfy your wants now rather than endure some discomfort for a future reward. You need to develop discipline.

The word *discipline* means "to delay gratification." You will only progress in life when you are willing to delay your gratification. Along with discipline there must be balancing. Balancing means you must let the lesser things die so that the greater may live.

4. Pursuit of Self-Interest. "God, I don't have time to do what You told me to do. Let me do my thing, and then I'll do Your thing." Instead of exploding with God's power, many people implode because they've become afraid, and they hold on tightly to what they've got, even though God isn't in it.

5. Spiritual Decay Within. Here's a principle that always works: You must defeat the devil or you're going to face him again. You can't just get him almost out. You can't be a little corrupt. Any little bit results in spiritual decay within. You sell your birthrights for trinkets. You sold your birthright for, "Baby, I love you. Just this once," or, "Hey, man, you're chicken. Everybody is doing it." Your birthrights are your confidence, your courage, your hope, your belief, your faith, your trust. These are things on the inside of you that birth the visions God gives you.

6. Lack of Motivation. Satan chips away your motivation in five ways.

- **Five Senses.** He gets your senses and emotions involved so that you "just don't feel like it."
- **Reasoning.** "I know God's will for me, but it doesn't make any logical sense." Remember, logic is in rebellion to faith. You can't get smarter than God.
- **Intellect.** If it's not popular with the Ph.D.s, you won't believe it. You confirm God's Word by what the scientists say, rather than confirming the scientists by what God's Word says.
- **Vain Imaginings.** You know what you have to do, but the enemy starts whispering, "You know what's going to happen if you try that. They'll laugh at you."
- **Memory.** The enemy whispers, "You remember the last time you tried that. You tried five times, and it didn't work. So don't even think about it again." He takes you back to the past, but God is the God of the NOW.

Right now look back at the five strategies you just read. Rank them in order from one to five, with one being the strategy that is most damaging to you personally, and five being the least damaging. I developed Vertical Leap training to neutralize those strategies, so keep reading.

How to Stop Being Sorry

God did not send you into the world to make a living. He sent you to change this world, to be the light on the hill, the salt of the earth. (See Matthew 5:13–14.) Out of the four hundred million sperm cells seeking one egg of the mother, 399,999,999 of them died. Only one made it, and it's you. You are God's greatest miracle. Nobody else can do what you do.

Within your DNA is a master code set by God from the beginning of time. This code is seen as the desires of your heart. "I will put My laws on their mind and write them on their hearts; and I will be their God, and they shall be My people" (Heb. 8:10). Man's flesh left to itself seeks to remain in homeostasis (balance of internal pressure). Life is the driving force of desire seeking fulfillment. Cathexis is desire unfulfilled, and frustration is defined as barriers to your goal.

God sent you here for a purpose, not to shrivel up into a molehill because of these barriers and frustrations, but to grow into a mountain. The cells of your body know by their DNA code where to go, when to arrive, how to bend, and how to cluster with like cells that form body parts. So too will God direct your steps to your destiny of purpose.

Most of us act as if we've just come to earth to

pay our house notes and car notes, go to sleep, wake up, and complain about our miserable lives and communities, and how somebody should do something. God sent *you* to do something. In order to achieve your purpose, you must have desire and be motivated.

Motivation

The desire/motivation formula is Desire • Habit • Incentive.

- **Desire.** Your motivation is ignited by your strong cravings, wants, and needs—desires. The Bible warns us in James 4 not to let lusts be our source of motivation. Lust is the outer drive, and it is reactionary to life's temptations. It is driven by what someone else has and not by God's plan encoded in our hearts as purpose (Heb. 8:10). God's Word should be your source of desire.
- **Habit.** Habits are actions taken without thought. Habits are birthed from successful repetitive actions. The strength of one's motivational force is dependent upon the habit of achieving the object or thing desired.
- **Incentive.** Incentive is the passion of desire. It strengthens the drive force of desire.

One can reasonably predict desire/motivation force mathematically by assigning numbers in a range of variance, that is, 1 = low motivation force to 10 = high motivation force. As an example, let's use a hungry person. He desires to eat. He has a choice between steak and vegetables. Which do you predict he will choose? Let's apply our desire/motivation formula.

Motivational Force (Hungry person example)				
Food available to a hungry person	Desire X *(Level of hunger)*	Habit X *(Habit of achieving desire)*	Incentive *(Level of passion for object desired)*	Motivational Force
Steak	10	5	10	500
Vegetable	10	5	3	150

Therefore, we can see that forecasting behavior is quite simple. Because he liked to eat steak (10) much more than vegetables (3) his motivational force to acquire steak was much higher. Notice if I were to change the habit of achieving desire from 5 to 0, there would be no motivation force (10 x 0 x 10 = 0). Or if I were to change the incentive to 0, there would be no motivation force (10 x 5 x 0 = 0). When we do not achieve our desires, it is due to poor habits of achieving our goals or due to having no incentives. God's mind in us (as expressed in Hebrews 8:10) is our inner incentive to move into His finished plan for our lives.

The Season for the Body of Christ

I've got good news. You don't need a bunch of collateral or a big down payment or a prestigious family name to become wealthy. In the twenty-first century, ideas are going to be worth more than an inheritance. People will pay millions for a good idea. The new technological world we're coming into is going to be the new affirmative action program, because it's going to put everyone on an equal plane. If you can dream it, there is somebody who can do it. The world will be hungry for dreams, visions, and ideas.

This is the season for the body of Christ. We're the ones with access to the most creative idea Source in the universe—God. We're the believers. God said in these latter days He would pour out His Spirit on all flesh. Young men would see visions and old men would dream dreams. (See Acts 2:17 and Joel 2:28.) He is preparing those of us with ears to hear and eyes to see as storehouses for the completion of His kingdom. God is raising up an apostolic people to dream and prepare the vision as architects of His kingdom coming.

I truly believe this is why you're reading this book. In order to fulfill your role in God's kingdom coming, you need to be equipped. That's the purpose of *Vertical Leap*. *Vertical Leap* has two dimensions. One is the personal success it enables you to achieve. The other is the working out of God's purposes on a global scale.

These are the guiding ideas behind the outreach to youth that my wife Hattie and I founded in 1977—B.O.S.S the Movement. We saw the dismal future that lay ahead for young people in the inner city and we decided "someone must do something, and the 'something' must be based on Christ and His Word." That's why B.O.S.S. stands for Building on Spiritual Substance. We have been successfully teaching young people ages seven to seventeen the relevance of God's Word in birthing their creative ideas from the spiritual realm to a physical reality. We received so many requests from adults for this teaching that we created what we now call Vertical Leap training (see page i for information on how you can attend). When an adult learns the Vertical Leap principles, we desire him or her to partner with B.O.S.S. the Movement to become a trainer in their local church or community.

I am telling you this right now so that you can understand there is more to be gained than your personal happiness. By birthing the dreams, visions, and ideas God gives you, you can be an agent for positive change on a global scale.

The next chapter will tell you how to understand your potential and to tap into its resources.

APPLICATION QUESTIONS

1. When was the last time you had to say "I'm sorry"?

   <u>When I jumped to conclusion</u>
   <u>and spoke to someone in an ungodly manner</u>

2. Do you want God to revive one of your dead dreams, or do you want Him to give you a new one?

   <u>Revive a dead dream</u>
   <u>Give me a new dream</u>

3. The five Satanic strategies for keeping us sorry are 1) fear, 2) weariness, 3) lack of discipline, 4) pursuit of self-interest, and 5) spiritual decay. Which one do you feel is most important to overcome in your life?

Weariness -
Lack of Discipline
Spiritual Decay

4. Do you have any pride issues that are keeping you from depending on God? Are you willing to sacrifice something that seems good in order to follow God's better calling? Explain.

Yes
Yes, I'm willing eating
unhealthy + smoking

5. What is the formula for motivational force? How would you rate your habit of achieving desire (on a scale of 1 to 10)?

Staying focus on Proverbs
18.16. I rate my habit
of achieving desire on
a scale of 8.

Chapter 2

Vertical Leap

Do you ever feel pushed around by life? Everything from your daily schedule to your life goals is dictated by the circumstances around you. How would you like to do the pushing for a change?

The law of cause and effect states that one's thinking is the cause and the result of his thinking is the effect. This law states that there is no such thing as luck. Man earns a living, behaves, and attracts things to him according to his self-concept (or his thinking).

Vertical Leap is about being the pusher instead of the pushed. It's about being proactive to the world around you, instead of reactive (visions on the inside creating the facts on the outside).

The best definition of Vertical Leap is this: Vertical Leap takes us from *facts to faith to action.* We start with the facts of our lives in the natural realm. For example, many of us feel lifeless and empty about our work. We are uncertain about God's purpose for our lives, let alone fulfilling it. Then we go to God's Word and we are imparted with faith about His purposes for the world, and we go to God in prayer and discover our role in His plans. Our faith results in taking action, and we see reality move from the spiritual realm to the material realm. That is the Vertical Leap—living on the basis of God's reality instead of our own perception of reality.

There are two foundational concepts you must master in order to take the Vertical Leap. They are 1) stay conscious and 2) do it NOW.

1. Stay conscious. Many of us go through days and weeks in an unconscious state. By that I mean that we are not thinking and so we fail to make right choices. We do not take advantage of the fact that God made us unique from all other creatures by giving us the ability to choose. Man is not a slave to stimulus-response as animals are.

If an animal is hungry, he'll eat. If he's sexually excited, he'll mate. It's part of his fleshly instinct. Animals do not have a choice. No lion thinks, "It isn't nice to kill this gazelle. Maybe I should morally look at his life. Does he have a family to feed?" The animal just wants to meet the need in his body.

Unfortunately, there are times that we humans act like animals. We sleep with other people's spouses because we have lust. We hurt other people to make ourselves more comfortable. But that isn't the best for us.

Remember, to make a Vertical Leap principle work, you've got to do two things: 1) stay conscious so that you make a decision based on God's Word instead of what your five senses tell you and 2) do it NOW so that you are moving when God moves.

A choice starts in the mind with your consciousness. You see, you can't make a choice without thinking or having an inner perception. *You can't do what you can't see.* You can't think or perceive without being conscious. So within my consciousness is my ability to choose. One can only be conscious NOW.

2. Do it NOW. NOW has been defined *as zero to five seconds.* NOW is the amount of time you can keep a thought, idea, or dream in short-term memory before it's embedded into long-term memory. (The average short-term memory span is two to five seconds.) NOW is the only place you can make a choice or decision. God is a God of NOW, and He communes with us NOW. NOW is all we have. We do not live in the past or the future. *We can only live and make choices in the NOW.*

We often try to figure out when God is going to move. God doesn't work according to our time lines. Your requirement is to stay ready and prayed up, for you never know when He may direct you. But when He speaks, do it NOW (zero to five seconds).

The enemy will have us do good things at the wrong times. Yesterday's good can be today's evil. Good is doing what God told you to do when He told you to do it. Peter in a vision saw a sheet lowered with what was previously considered unclean animals. Yet, the angel of the Lord instructed Peter to eat. The angel explained, "What God has cleansed, you must not call common. (Acts 10). Don't look at things the way things used to be. Look at the way God is revealing them to you now. Peter had to upgrade his map to reality.

Faith is NOW. Facts are in the past.

Your Potential

The Vertical Leap is designed to purify and maximize your potential. *Your potential is made up of word perceptions, which are words spoken and unspoken, that influence your thoughts, feelings, attitudes, actions, and beliefs.* These five things determine whether you will give birth to a vision from God or say I'm sorry once again. In other words, your potential creates your reality.

We need to recognize that our potential is under our power to control. If our feelings, attitudes, actions, and beliefs are hindering us from success, we can change them by changing our thinking. We change our thinking by changing our sensory perceptions. What we give our attention to comes to live in us as our thought life (Prov. 23:7).

It's very important to see the chain of events that starts with word perceptions: Word perceptions shape my thinking; my thinking shapes my feelings; my feelings shape my attitudes and actions; my repeated actions form my beliefs; my beliefs become my potential and my potential shapes my presuppositions (how I presuppose the world to be). A presupposition is a thought that has been reinforced. Presuppositions are dangerous because they are self-perpetuating. Whatever the heart embraces as true the mind will support.

Potential —View 1

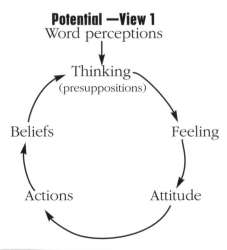

Word perceptions

↓

Thinking
(presuppositions)

Beliefs   Feeling

Actions   Attitude

If I think "I'm sleepy, I feel tired," I will take on the attitude and actions of one who is tired. My actions repeated become my belief. That belief reinforces how I see the world (presupposition). How I see the world reinforces my thinking—positively or negatively.

It starts small, but it gets big and creates reality. It can start in your childhood with positive or negative words spoken by your parents or an authority figure that shaped your thinking by you embracing their words as truth. You have responded over and over again to these words. Now you are where you are.

Here's an example. Your second grade teacher said, "You're not good at math," so you start thinking, "I'm not good at math" (thinking). The word perceptions have changed your thinking. You feel stupid (feelings). You begin to hate going to math classes (attitude). You don't even bother to study for math tests because you're "not good at math" (actions). When you fail your math tests you conclude, "I'll never be good enough at math." (belief/potential). "And I won't apply for a job that requires math because they will see I'm not qualified" (presupposition).

That was the first round in the chain of events. Now you enter all situations in life with the presupposition: I will never be good at math. Whatever the heart embraces as true, the mind will support.

Let's continue the example with math. Say you grow up and get a job in sales. You're good at talking to people, so you get a lot of sales. But you're always in trouble with your boss because the math in your reports is inaccurate. When he encourages you to improve, you think, "That's it. I'm going to lose my job because I'm not good at math" (thinking). You feel depressed (feelings). You dread going to work (attitude) and avoid your boss (actions). Finally, when you're fired, a new presupposition emerges: "I'll never be able to keep a good job."

Potential—View 2

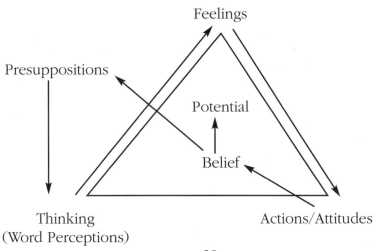

Do you see how a negative word that captured your attention started the chain of events? However, a change of thinking at any point would have stopped the negative power of that word. (Vertical Leap will help you realize a change of thinking.)

Can you identify some presuppositions in your life? Remember, a presupposition is thinking that has been reinforced through the chain of events that make up potential. Try to think of one good presupposition and one bad one, and write them in the margin of this book. For example, I'm an organized person (positive). I'm not creative (negative).

To rejuvenate your potential, change your thinking NOW. Say to yourself, "I am creative." The next chance you have to be creative, jump on it! In Romans 12:2 God says He will renew your mind through His Word. Don't look to the past to define your thinking. Looking back to determine your forward potential is extremely limiting.

Remember, your feelings, attitude, actions, and beliefs are *your choice* based on *your thinking NOW.* No one can limit your potential and corrupt your presuppositions without your cooperation. Change the words and thought perceptions you embrace as true and you change your destiny.

Redemption

Adam and Eve were the first to have their potential corrupted. In Genesis 2 mankind was in their proper place in the garden—no sickness, no lack, perfectly following God, no fear. Their reality was driven by the mind of God. They walked with Him in the garden and thought His thoughts.

In their original state they had full charge of their birthrights. Every person is born with these birthrights—*confidence, courage, hope, belief, faith, and trust in God as his source.*

But in Genesis 3 they were bamboozled by the serpent and decided to listen to Satan's words. They chose based on their logic instead of God's word. (Remember, logic based on the five senses is in rebellion to faith.) When they moved away from the word of God, they fell into the flesh, and they died spiritually. They lost their birthrights, and their presuppositions about encountering God changed. Instead of looking forward to walking with Him in the cool of the evening, they were in fear (Gen. 3:10).

God made a way of redemption available for us through the death of His Son, Jesus. Redemption is a thing being in its proper place, taken out of place, and restored to its place again. Vertical Leap is about redemption—regaining our ability to be moved by the Word of God unto perception on the inside instead of our senses and voices of others on the outside.

How to Use This Book

I am so excited about how a Vertical Leap can change your life. My only regret in you reading this book is that I will not be present to witness the transformation that will take place in you. If this book has touched you, please contact us. We would like to hear from you (Remember, you are also invited to attend a Vertical Leap seminar to receive more in depth training. See page i for more information.)

To help you mentally organize what causes a Vertical Leap, I've created the diagram on this page.

Vertical Leap

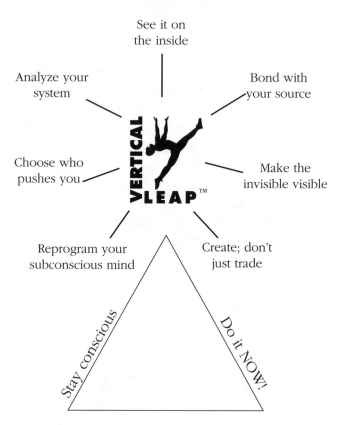

At the bottom, holding everything up, you'll recognize the two principles we just discussed—stay conscious and do it NOW. I cannot emphasize enough that for the rest of this book to be effective you must put these words into action.

Unconscious people who wait are no threat to Satan and no help to God.

See how the seven spiritual principles are organized around the words *Vertical Leap* like spokes on a wheel? That's because they all contribute to making the Vertical Leap possible.

Because these principles are based on Gestalt thinking (each principle stands independent of need for support of the other principles), you don't start at the top and work your way around the circle. You don't even have to complete one principle before moving on to the next. In reality you will probably work on all the principles simultaneously. As they interact together you will realize the Vertical Leap in different areas of your life.

Notice that I said a Vertical Leap can occur in more than one area of your life. In my teaching I use a lot of examples from business, but I also include the application for personal life. That's because principles cross over in every area of life. Principles are truths. You do not put a truth in a box because everything is interconnected with truth, and it leads back to who is the truth—Jesus. If it is not interconnected and interwoven, it is not the truth. So a business principle can also apply to your marriage or church.

It is helpful to compare principles to facts. Principles are spiritual truths and do not change. Facts are subject to change. Principles create and can change facts.

So whenever you read the word *principle* in this book, pay special attention because that principle can transform your life and change your negative facts.

The other important thing to keep in mind

about these principles is that they are spiritual. Their operation does not depend on your own might. It depends on your willingness to trust in the power of God.

Now here's your first chance to practice what you've learned so far. Stay conscious! Don't put this book down because your brain is starting to feel strained. Make a decision to keep reading because the next chapter contains the first spiritual principle—see it on the inside. Do it NOW!

APPLICATION QUESTIONS

1. In order to take a Vertical Leap you must 1) stay conscious and 2) do it NOW. Think of a situation you encounter regularly where you need to stay conscious and make a thinking decision rather than just react to a stimulus.

   Developing web pages

   Being a good steward

   over my finaces

2. You have the power to shape your potential by choosing how you think about yourself. Were there negative words in your childhood? Identify some of those words now and make a decision to change your thinking on those issues.

   I will not be a smoker
   I will not be single all my life
   I will not be in debt

3. With which birthrights are every person born?

   faith, confidence, courage, hope, belief, trust in God as my source

4. Explain in your own words how the idea of redemption is similar to the idea of Vertical Leap.

   Redemption is something being in its rightful place and taken out of place + restored to its proper designation
   Vertical Leap – standing on the word of God, seeing things as though it was + belief / faith on the inner parts (mind, heart) + ignoring any words that is not of God.

Part 2

Seven Spiritual Principles

Chapter 3

Principle #1
See It on the Inside

A sk yourself, *Is this book I'm reading really here?* Your answer is most probably yes. The existence of the book is a reality that you perceived with your five senses.

Now ask yourself, *What does God want me to be doing in five years?* The answer to that question is a truth that cannot be perceived through the five senses. It must be perceived on the inside through the written Word of God and/or the voice of the Spirit of God.

Has our reality been fully shaped by God's Word? Not yet. That's because we *hear* God's Word without having a clear *perception* of it.

To help you understand perception, let me give you an example. "Go get some *keechie keechie.*"

Can you do it? No. That's because you have no inward perception of keechie keechie. You brain is saying, *Seeking, seeking, seeking. File not found. Need more data.* To create an inward perception you need to associate keechie keechie with something you know.

What if I tell you keechie keechie is like *kaatchie kaatchie?* "Now, get it!" You still can't do it because there's no inward perception. But what if I tell you that kaatchie kaatchie is like banana?

Now, what color is keechie keechie? Yellow, that's right. You knew the answer because you had an inward perception of banana.

What I'm saying is this: You cannot perform an action toward your reality on the outside unless you have perception on the inside of you. You can't do what your mind can't see.

The Battle Is in the Mind

There's a battle taking place: a battle between those things on the outside of us, reality perceived by the five senses, versus those things on the inside, truth from the Spirit of God. Will your reality be defined from the *outside in* or the *inside out?* Are you going to be reactive to life, pushed from the outside? If so, you will be angry and bitter and blame people for jerking you around on the outside and making you feel inferior on the inside.

When you feel inferior on the inside, you lose power on the outside. We want to have power on the inside so we can change the outside. We want to push the inside out. That's the Vertical Leap. "As [a man] thinketh in his heart, so is he" (Prov. 23:7, KJV).

You are going to do unto others what you want them to do to you. But you're going to do it first. God so loved the world that He gave first (John 3:16). He was proactive.

Jesus didn't wait for conditions on the outside to affect Him on the inside. He already had an agenda on the inside because He only did what His Father showed Him to do John 8:28–29. He heard in His heart, and it became truth and reality.

Jesus (The Word unto perception—reality) is the truth. (See John 1.) So if the reality you perceive on the outside is in opposition to God's Word in your heart, it's a lie.

Logic rebels against faith. Jesus healed the sick and raised the dead. That's not logical, but He did it. He had the habit of trusting His Father. Jesus was habitually addicted to obeying God's Word.

You can't serve both logic and God's Word. When the multitude needed feeding, Jesus multiplied five loaves and two fishes. That was not logical. Jesus walked on water. He defied the law of physics. Peter walked on water, too, until he got logical and looked at the waves. Then he sank.

Voodoo puts a word curse on people. If you embrace the words to be true, the mind will support it, and you will receive the curse based on your level of belief in its evil power.

If we embrace God's Word as true, we will have abundant life based on our level of faith (Matt. 9:29).

Hierarchy of Existence

Now that you see the difference between perceiving reality on the inside versus reality on the outside, I need to stretch your faith a little bit with a new concept.

In this section I'm going to explain a hierarchy of existence in a way you've probably never heard before. I want to begin by giving you a principle: Out of the greater flows the lesser. (Remember, principles apply universally, so pay special attention to them.) This principle may seem unclear now, but it will make sense soon.

Below is a diagram of this hierarchy. The diagram would be expressed in words this way (starting from the bottom). Things exist within space. Space exists within time. Time exists within consciousness. Consciousness exists within man. Man exists within God.

Hierarchy of Existence

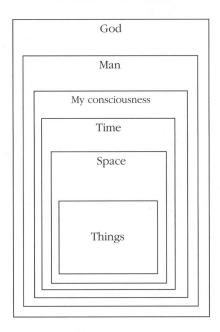

God

Man

My consciousness

Time

Space

Things

So, again, out of the greater (God) flows the lesser (me, my consciousness and so on). Do you also notice how time, space, and things all exist within consciousness? This may be hard to accept at first, but you can see it if you think about it.

First of all, think about time and consciousness. When you have a five-minute conversation with a friend, you have given him five minutes of your conscious time. Time is a measurement of one's conscious awareness; therefore, it is in one's consciousness that time is observed as a measuring tool. A dead man is not conscious of time.

Now let's look at the relationship between space and time. In order for objects to be differentiated, there must be space that separates them. The space between objects is the distance from one object to another. This distance of space can be measured by time. Therefore space exists within conscious time measurement.

Finally, the easy one. Within space exists all of the things we perceive with our five senses: you, me, chair, car, tree, house, and so on. All things that exist in the three-dimensional earth do so within time and space, and they exist within my conscious awareness that exists within me.

So you can see how within my consciousness exists time, space, and things. The Word of God points out that the kingdom of God is within us (Luke 17:21). So often we look outside of ourselves for things that really exist on the inside of us. I try to get things from you when I can find them within myself. I blame you when I should look at what's wrong within me.

We chase dreams and visions on the outside when God wants us to return to the inside. "Seek

ye first the kingdom of God, and his righteousness; and all these things shall be added unto you"
(Matt. 6:33, KJV). All things are made up of Him.
Colossians 1:16–17 says everything that was made
was made by the Word of God. Out of the invisible are birthed material things. God is the One
who supplies visions, dreams, and ideas for us to
birth as things into the world.

Parallel Universes

There's another important distinction between
inner truth and outer reality. Outer reality is limited
to the past, but God's inner reality brings perception of the NOW that forms the future. "Greater is
he that is in you, than he that is in the world" (1
John 4:4, KJV). God gives foreknowledge of things
not yet seen.

Usually entrepreneurs operate with some kind
of foreknowledge. An entrepreneur is one who
takes calculated risks for private profit. An entrepreneur sees something on the inside that has not
been birthed on the outside, and he works to
bring it to pass.

In the natural, we move through life from left to
right. In other words, we see things occur chronologically: we're born, grow to adulthood, have our
own children, grow old, and eventually die. It's a
fantastic thing to know that God isn't bound by
left to right chronological thinking. He sees our
lives from right to left as preexisting possibilities.
When you're starting something, God already
knows how it finishes. What better reason to seek
His voice on the inside!

We are dealing with predestination here. The

Word says God has "blessed us [past tense] with all spiritual blessings in heavenly places in Christ: According as he hath chosen us in him before the foundation of the world, that we should be holy and without blame before him in love: Having predestinated us unto the adoption of children by Jesus Christ to himself, according to the good pleasure of his will" (Eph. 1:3–5, KJV).

God has already finished everything we've started. He has finished it in the spirit realm, in heaven, and you're seeking it on earth.

Jesus told the disciples to pray: "Our father which art in heaven, Hallowed be thy name. Thy kingdom come. Thy will be done in earth, *as it is* in heaven" (Matt. 6:9–10, KJV, italics added).

I believe Jesus was talking about parallel universes—the kingdom of earth and the kingdom of heaven. In heaven God can see the finish and the start. The Bible tells us to pray that God's heavenly kingdom will manifest on earth (unfolding left to right chronologically) as it is already manifested in heaven. "Thy will be done in earth, *as it is* [present-tense] in heaven" (Matt. 6:10, KJV, italics added).

The next diagram compares God's predestined timeline to man's logical timeline. If you want to be in the zone where God blesses, then you must choose (free will) to line up with God's already finished will.

In the diagram, God wanted that person to go to college when he was eighteen, but he waited until he was twenty-four. He was behind God. Then he started a business when he was forty-one when God's perfect time was forty-five. He got ahead of God.

God's Timeline vs. Man's Timeline

4th Dimension Heaven							Supernatural
15 yrs	20 yrs.	25 yrs.	30 yrs.	35 yrs.	40 yrs.	45 yrs.	50 yrs.

Behind God (Going to college)

In time with God (Marriage)

Ahead of God (Starting a business)

Anointing

The "Zone"

3rd Dimension Earth							Human
15 yrs.	20 yrs.	25 yrs.	30 yrs.	35 yrs.	40 yrs.	45 yrs.	50 yrs.

When you have a bicycle chain that isn't lined up with the sprockets, it will slip and spin and the tire won't turn. Many of us are working our tails off, but we're spinning because we are not in sync with God's finished timing.

In the diagram, the person *was* in sync with God's timing for marriage at thirty-two years old. During that time, he was in the "zone," under the anointing.

Think about your life right now. Do you think you are in sync with God's timing? If you find out you're behind God's timeline and you make a choice to line up with Him, you become in "right standing" with God immediately; however, past choices can contaminate new possibilities. There are wages to be paid for sin and for righteousness.

If you want to be anointed, your prayer should be, "Thy will be done. God, let me be on time with what You have already predestined for me." The problem is most of us are trying to get God to line up with us, rather than spending enough time with Him so that we line up with what He wants us to do.

It's easy to say that we want to hear God's voice on the inside, but some of us don't understand what we need to do in order to recognize His voice. The next spiritual nugget—Bond With Your Source—will explain in real terms how to know God's voice.

APPLICATION QUESTIONS

1. You can allow your reality to be determined one of two ways: from the *outside in,* or from the *inside out.* Which way do you usually allow your reality to be defined? What is the result?

   _____

   _____

   _____

   _____

2. This chapter states that you can't serve both logic and God's Word. In your own words, explain why.

   _____

   _____

   _____

3. Do you think your timeline is in sync with God's timeline? If you're not sure how to answer, pray about it.

_____

_____

_____

_____

_____

Chapter 4

Principle #2
Bond With Your Source

Do you know what it feels like to have a good friend with whom you can talk at any time about any thing? How did your relationship get to that point? You spent time with each other and shared your heart. You shared experiences, perhaps hard times. You bonded together so that when one speaks the other understands.

This chapter will tell you how to bond with God. Remember, He has predestined what we want. He gives dreams, visions, and ideas to guide us.

In this chapter you will come to understand levels of bonding, methods of bonding, what happens when you don't bond, and examples of bonding from Scripture.

Four Levels of Bonding

Bonding with God, or anyone, requires that one moves through four progressive levels—1) sacrifice, 2) relational bonding, 3) perceptible bonding, and 4) material bonding.

1. Sacrifice. Mechanical physics introduces to us the law of cost. Nothing is free. Someone or something must pay the price for another to gain. Jesus paid the price for our salvation so that we could be children of God. Salvation is free to you and me, but it cost Jesus His life. The Bible is filled with examples of patriarchs who sacrificed greatly to bond with God.

2. Relational Bonding. At this stage, one's sacrificial giving has resulted in a relational bond of trust. Relational bonding comes as one gains knowledge through personal experience. Jesus desired to bond with mankind, and He paid the highest price so that we may be relationally bonded with Him. I challenge you to look through the Bible and see saint after saint who sacrificed in order to be relationally bond with God. The relational bond is strengthened by the amount of time and attention invested in relationships.

3. Perceptible Bonding. Spending time together and developing a bonding relationship, we learn to recognize God's voice as He speaks to us through dreams, visions, and ideas. We have God's mind in us so we can perceive what He is saying. We see things as God sees them. After living and struggling with someone for a long time, you start to think and see life the way they do. *Whatever you give your attention to, it's spirit will come to live in you.*

41

4. Material Bonding. When we bond with God we gain everything He has. When my wife Hattie and I were dating, what I had didn't belong to her. However, when we became bonded as husband and wife, everything I had became hers.

When you have perceptibly bonded with God, He will draw unto you the things that you need. I call this the corridor principle: As a man moves in accordance with God's plan, he draws to himself the desires of his heart. The scriptural foundation for the corridor principle is Matthew 6:33: "Seek ye first the kingdom of God, and his righteousness; and all these things shall be added unto you" (KJV).

Ask yourself, *What level of bonding do I have with my Source?* If you are not sure that you have a relational bond, please turn to the back of this book and read the page titled *How to Know You Are a Child of God* (Appendix C). It's the most important thing you can do for yourself right now.

Perhaps you have a relational bond, but you haven't grown any further in the Lord. The next section tells how to make the perceptible bond.

Creating the Perceptible Bond

Many of us don't have a perceptible bond with God. We've sacrificed and spent enough time to have a relational bond with Him, but not enough time to recognize His voice. When God calls us to obedience, we often respond with fear because something has to be sacrificed for this bond to occur.

We see sacrifice for the first time in Genesis 3

when an animal was killed for man's covering. This was a foreshadowing of man's relationship to God being restored.

Abraham was honored among men because he was willing to sacrifice his son. Before Solomon was granted great wealth and wisdom, he presented God with a huge sacrifice. (See 2 Chronicles 1:1–12.) Scripture repeatedly shows that sacrifice precedes great blessings from God.

The sacrifice God most wants is our conscious attention. Attention means worship, which has two aspects of meaning: 1) narrowing our focus of consciousness to the exclusion of other things, and 2) expressing exaggerated respect to a divine object or being. Remember, you have to stay conscious to think and bond with God. Worship also requires giving up our time and attention.

Does God want us to bond with Him because He is empty? No. God has everything and needs nothing. He wants to bond because a father desires to bond with his children.

Our motivation to bond is really selfish. It's not about us giving to God; it's about God giving to us. God fills us with the foundational substance that makes up all things: confidence, courage, hope, belief, faith, and trust in Him. Without these spiritual substances actively working in us nothing would be made that is made. Man would cease to exist.

Remember, whatever I give my attention to, it's spirit comes to live in me. If you look at pornography, that spirit comes to live in you. If you watch sitcoms and soap operas, that spirit comes to live in you.

If you give a lot of your attention to a person,

you will start to think and act like that person. Their spirit becomes a part of you.

Whatever you join your "members" to becomes your master (1 Cor. 6:15, KJV). I can tell what you love by what you spend your free time doing.

Think about this past week. Who or what got your time? Now I know that a certain amount of time is consumed by working, eating, sleeping— things you have to do to survive. But how did you choose to use the time that was under your control?

Your spirit lives or dies based on what you do with your time. The principle of biogenesis simply suggests that organisms reproduce after their own kind. Your spirit body is like your physical body. Your physical body came from dirt, so it must partake of that which it came out of to live. In other words, you must feed it physical food. When I eat a hamburger, I am ultimately eating something that came out of dirt.

As a spirit body you also need to partake of that which you came out of to live—the very Word/breath of God. Our food of the spirit is the Word of God. If we don't eat of the Word of God we will die spiritually. Remember, to live you must remain in what you came out of. What is in Him will live in you.

God wants you to give your attention to Him and His Word because He has what you need. If you keep Him on your mind, you will prosper because He *is* prosperity. "Now therefore, listen to me, my children pay attention to the words of my mouth" (Prov. 7:24, NKJV).What is in Him will go into you.

The most important way to give God attention is

worship. *Worship* is defined by the dictionary as "extravagant respect, admiration, or devotion to a person or object." The extravagant part refers to sacrifice—of your energy, awareness, and focus. You select God to the exclusion of all others. Isaiah wrote, "Thou wilt keep him in perfect peace, whose mind is stayed on thee" (Isa. 26:3, KJV).

Remember our two key concepts—consciousness and NOW. You must stay conscious to worship God because worship requires an active mind. And you must worship Him *NOW* (zero to five seconds) because He's a God of the NOW.

Worship is being aware of all the things God is doing. You are so focused, attentive, aware, and conscious, that you are sensitive to the Spirit of God's movement (John 4:24). The Israelites had to be aware when the fire by day and cloud by night moved. Are you aware when the Spirit moves?

God will not accept half-hearted respect. Cain's sacrifice was rejected because he did not sacrifice what God required (Gen. 4:1-6).

God is jealous for our worship. Jealousy is defined as intolerant of rivalry or unfaithfulness; vigilant in guarding a possession. When you enter God's presence and your thoughts wander, you are creating rivals to His presence.

He's jealous about our worship because He wants a good connection to you. If there's a blockage in worship, will you get the purity of God's purpose and plan? No. That's why He's jealous about the hookup. He doesn't want anything to subvert your relationship with Him. Through worship, God wants to show us His timeline for our lives.

God fills us up with Himself when we worship. He makes us children of God, which means He puts His nature in us. God's nature is to overflow. When you have everything and He keeps giving you more, then you overflow. When your overflow of God's nature reaches others, then you know God is in you. So if love and giving is flowing into you, then you will overflow love and giving.

What If You're Not Bonded?

It's easy to tell when the bond is not strong enough for us to recognize His voice. In that situation, we have no passion for His purpose for our lives. Because we have no passion, we take no action, and we get negative feedback. We form negative habits, which in turn form a negative character. That negative character forms a negative destiny that will crystallize into negative circumstances all around us. Our potential is wasted because we did not move by the Word of God. We moved by our old paradigms.

Enemies all around us are coming to do war in our minds, causing us to feel, "I can't. I'm not worthy. I should just give up." If we spend all our time with the world, when it comes time to step out in faith we don't have enough in our potential to do it. We are weak and powerless. We can't stand up and gird ourselves.

Wherever there is a lack of bonding there will also be a spirit of manipulation. People will cry, they'll fight, they'll buffalo, they'll cheat, and they'll steal to get their needs met (James 1).

Bonding with God will birth trust. I don't have

to manipulate God because I trust Him. Where there is bonding, there will be trust, power, and anointing.

When you trust God, then you can act when you hear His voice. Faith moves without physical evidence. The act of responding in faith (taking action) produces the evidence on the outside. That is where most Christians fall down. They say, "God, give me money, and then I'll do what You tell me to do." The Israelites did the same thing. "God give us water, give us things, and then we'll worship You." God wants us to worship Him so that He can impart to us the wisdom to get our needs met. It is in worship that we learn to trust Him—to do what He says to do. We must learn to trust God's Word unto perception on the inside more than the things of the world on the outside.

Those who take calculated risks and step out are those who have made the decision to trust God more than their feelings, more than what they see. It takes courage to be a man of faith. You need to be prepared to fall. Matthew 10:39 says, "If you cling to your life, you will lose it; but if you give it up for me, you will save it" (TLB).

God is looking for someone who doesn't hold on to his own life. He must be willing to die. There must be something you're willing to die for in order to have the capacity to live by faith.

Heroes of Faith

I always get so inspired when I read Hebrews 11, which lists the heroes of faith. These people had real attitude. Some of us say we walk by faith, but we don't have a faith attitude. A problem comes up and we give up. We need to say, "I am going to overcome this fact by my faith attitude."

It was by having a faith attitude that Abel obeyed God and brought an offering that pleased God more than Cain's offering did (Heb. 11:4). When Abel brought his offering to God his gift represented the right attitude. Some of us do things for God, but we have bad attitudes. God doesn't want your bad attitudes. (See Isaiah 1:10–20.)

When God gives you a dream or vision, it may look foolish to everyone around you. That's when you need an attitude like Noah's.

"Noah was another who trusted God. When he heard God's warning about the future, Noah believed him even though there was then no sign of a flood, and wasting no time, he built the ark and saved his family. Noah's belief in God was in direct contrast to the sin and disbelief of the rest of the world—which refused to obey—and because of his faith he became one of those whom God has accepted" (Heb. 11:7, TLB).

Can you imagine Noah's attitude, being able to build this ark for 120 years with no rain and people laughing at him. He must have had an awesome attitude! Abraham was another man who looked crazy when he followed God.

"Abraham trusted God, and when God told him to leave home and go far away to another land which he promised to give him, Abraham obeyed. Away he went . . ." (Heb. 11:8, TLB).

Abraham left Ur of the Chaldees. In today's terms, he left Las Vegas and headed into the desert. He lived in a well-established city with all the conveniences and packed up to go to no man's land. He saw the Word of God alive on the inside.

"Sarah, too, had faith, and because of this she was able to become a mother inspite of her old age, for she realized that God, who gave her his promise, would certainly do what he said. And so a whole nation came from Abraham, who was too old to even have one child—a nation with so many millions of people that, like the stars of the sky and the sand of the ocean shores, there is no way to count them. These men of faith I have mentioned died without ever receiving all that God had promised them; but they saw it all awaiting them on ahead and were glad" (Heb. 11:11–13, TLB).

We're seeing generation building here. It's not about what you have now. You have to have a generational, life-building picture. You're going to have to think bigger. We think only about ourselves. God has a picture of NOW, but it's for the generations to come. We may just be one part of the torch-bearing. That's why my goal is for every adult who completes Vertical Leap training to turn around and become a trainer for youth in B.O.S.S. the Movement. (For more information about B.O.S.S., see page 179.)

"While God was testing him, Abraham still trusted in God and his promises, and so he offered up his son Isaac, and was ready to slay him on the altar of sacrifice; yes, to slay even Isaac, through whom God had promised to give Abraham a whole nation of descendants! He believed that if Isaac died God would bring him back to life again; and that is just about what happened, for as far as Abraham was concerned, Isaac was doomed to death, but he came back again alive!" (Heb. 11:17–19, TLB).

Abraham was willing to sacrifice the son he loved to God. He loved Him more than anything. Abraham gave God his maximum attention. God will test us. If you put something above Him, He's going to find out if you would sacrifice it. When we start putting each other before God, He will tell you, "It's time to put this thing to the test. Who do you love more?"

"It was [a faith attitude] that brought the walls of Jericho tumbling down after the people of Israel had walked around them seven days as God had commanded them" (Heb. 11:30, TLB).

Did those people have attitude to march around the city seven times and blow a trumpet and shout? What kind of faith attitude is in our churches/communities? Is it kick back and sit on our soft pews? God is looking at our attitude. This book is about giving you an attitude that will change your communities for the better.

Hebrews 11 lists many others who trusted God and acted out their faith attitude—Isaac, Joseph, Moses, Rahab, Gideon, Barak, Samson, Jacob, David, and Samuel.

All of these people moved without knowing the end of their moment. They did not see with their physical eyes, but they had a foreknowledge of God's Word. They took calculated risks because they had bonded with their God. They knew they could trust Him, no matter what the facts said. They took the Vertical Leap.

How to Know if You're Called by God

The examples from Hebrews 11 illustrate three ways you can know that God has called you.

Sign #1. You are driven out of your comfort zone. To be in your comfort zone, you're in logic. God takes away what seems to be logical, so that you have to move by faith (Matt. 10). This is a preparation step. Whatever happens will be by His Spirit in His time, and you'll just have to be patient.

God is looking for people who are willing to step out of their comfort zones. You have to give up something to get something. When I am weak in this area, my wife, Hattie, becomes stronger.

Even Jesus was sent out of His comfort zone before He began His public ministry (Luke 4:1). Right after the Holy Spirit descended on Him, God sent Him to be tempted in the desert.

God drove many people in Scripture out of their comfort zones. The children of Israel had to leave Egypt to go through the desert. Paul was knocked off his horse and blinded on the road to Damascus. Noah was told to build a ship unlike anything he had ever known. Joseph was asked to take a wife who was pregnant with a child that was not his own.

To put it in today's words, when God calls, you have to leave your "'hood" and go into another territory. God is breaking up old clusters and forming new ones.

Sign #2. You are rendered helpless and dependent on others. When you say, "God use me," be careful. His thoughts are not your thoughts (Isa. 55:8).

51

When you are forced to depend totally on God—instead of money—you find yourself sincerely asking, "Am I in Your will?" and really listening for the answer.

In the past you may have judged people on welfare and now here you are in line doing the welfare shuffle. You used to say, "Get a job like everybody else," and now you can't find a job. You are dependent on God's grace through others to help you.

Sign #3. You experience a dark time of the soul and are misunderstood by those around you. This is when you are at the limit of your physical and emotional strength. The devil shows up and tempts you to break covenant with God. He may entice you to lie, steal, or cheat. In other words, he gets you to doubt God's ability to help you. If you fail the test your despair becomes deeper and darker. But if you pass the test by trusting God and remain a worshipper, you get promoted and will often lead others through the areas of your tempting. God can trust you for you are dead to self and have bonded with Him. "No longer I who live, but Christ lives in me" (Gal. 2:20, NKJV).

When you're bonded with God, you will hear His voice on the inside, and experience His call, then spiritual principle #3 is what you need to move forward. It's called "Make the Invisible Visible." This is one of my favorite principles because it highlights again that with God you can start with nothing and accomplish great things.

APPLICATION QUESTIONS

1. What you give your attention to, its spirit comes to live in you. According to how your spend your time, what spirits do you think are living in you right now?

_____

_____

_____

2. When you overflow with the attributes of God's nature (such as love and giving) then you know God is in you. What attributes of God overflow from you?

_____

_____

3. Have you ever tried to manipulate God? What was the result?

_____

_____

4. How could your dream from God impact generations to come?

_____

_____

Chapter 5

Principle #3
Make the Invisible Visible

Have you ever been around someone who has lost hope? Hopelessness comes in all kinds of situations: serious illness, abusive spouse, rebellious children, a dead-end job, bankruptcy.

Does a person without hope do anything to improve their situation? No. But we know that as long as there is a God, there is hope.

When God speaks His word into us, it comes in the form of hope. The purpose of hope is to become a thing. When God gives you hope, or a desire, in your heart, that is His embryo of reality. Many of us abort God's desires because we don't feel capable of delivering them.

This chapter is about how you get from having a hope, which is invisible, to having a thing, which is tangible (in short, hope to a thing). I will give you two different ways of accomplishing hope to a thing. One is a series of steps and the other is an algebraic equation. Finally, I will teach you how to win the battle in the spiritual dimension that is trying to steal your hope in the physical dimension.

Steps of Hope to a Thing

When you seek God for dreams, visions, and ideas, He will often respond by giving you hope. Next, you take action to change your hope to a thing. You may want to follow these three basic steps.

I would like to suggest that you think of a hope in your life right now. It doesn't have to be your life goal—just a step toward that goal. As you read these steps and look at the diagram, think about how you would apply them to your hope.

1. Decide to believe. Make a conscious decision to embrace the hope and believe that it will come to pass. In order to believe, you need to have trust in the source of your hope. That's what principle #2—bonding with your source—was all about.

When you have hope, you say, "I wish I had that bus." But when you believe, you say, "That's my bus."

The best way to change hope to belief is to look at what the source of your hope has done in the past. I call this *touchstoning* (remembering God's goodness, His track record). The idea of touchstoning comes from the Old Testament. When God moved on behalf of His people, they would mark the place with a pile of stones. Then every time they went back to that place they would remember what God had done.

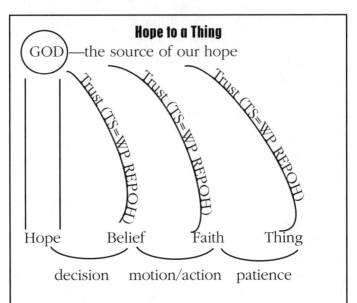

Hope to a Thing

GOD—the source of our hope

Hope — Belief — Faith — Thing

decision — motion/action — patience

Trust in the source of your hope is the key to turning your hope to a thing. One comes to trust God as his/her source of hope by touchstoning (TS=Remembering God's goodness.) God called man to worship and praise (WP) Him repetitiously (REPOH) until touchstoning forms a good habit of trusting Him. We must trust God to: make a *decision* to believe our *hope*; *act* on our *belief* so that *faith* is manifested; and be *patient* until our faith becomes a *material thing*.

For example, after the Lord appeared to Jacob in a dream and promised to bless him, Jacob "took the stone that he had put for his pillows, and set it up for a pillar, and poured oil upon the top of it" (Gen. 28:18, KJV).

Another good example is when Joshua and the people of Israel saw God stop the waters of the

Jordan River with an invisible dam. Joshua told a representative from each of the twelve tribes of Israel to take a stone from the middle of the dry riverbed and carry it to shore. They piled up the stones as a monument to what God had done. Joshua explained, "In the future . . . when your children ask you why these stones are here and what they mean, you are to tell them that these stones are a reminder of this amazing miracle—that the nation of Israel crossed the Jordan River on dry ground!" (Josh. 4:21–22, TLB).

David built up stones of remembrance by writing the Book of Psalms.

We go to our own stones of remembrance through touchstoning, which I define as remembering God's goodness in worship and praise repetitiously. Remember what He has already done for you. This builds trust in God as the source of your hope. Trust says, "He is able, willing, and will do it for me."

How long do you touchstone? Repetitiously—until you trust God enough to believe in the hope He gave you. So if I can't believe, then my level of trust is too low, and I need to touchstone more. Study the Word of God and remind yourself that He is able, willing, and will do it for *me* as He did it for *them.*

2. Take action on your belief. Action will bring you up from belief to faith. Faith is belief in action. Now you have given your hope visibility. Action takes more trust than just mentally believing, so you need to keep touchstoning (keep worshipping and praising, keep remembering His track record) until you can trust enough to take the necessary action.

3. Be patient. The patience stage is really time for a lot of touchstoning because you need to trust your Source even when nothing seems to be happening.

I am going through the patience stage right now. God told Hattie and me to build the Alhatti Christian Resort, a lovely resort in Idyllwild, California, where Christians have a place to retreat and spend time with God. God provided prime real estate in the tall, whispering pines of the San Jacinto Mountains above Palm Springs. We built private cottages, a women's dorm, men's dorm, conference rooms, and an elegant dining area. There is also a state-of-the-art recording studio, an outdoor chapel, amphitheater, stocked lake, spa, sports courts, and walking trails. We conduct four-day Vertical Leap Seminars there every month (see page 180 for information on how you can attend). Our vision is to have Christians from all over the country gather at the Alhatti Christian Resort for rest, group conferences, spiritual training, and ministry impartation. This facility is dedicated to serving the body of Christ.

We've built the resort, but we have not seen it used to full capacity. Financially, it's in the red. But while the books are out of balance on the resort, God brings the needed resources through our successful secular business. A multimillion-dollar contract here, a million-dollar contract there. We had hope, belief, and took action to build the Alhatti Christian Resort—now we're in the patience stage.

Patience is something you learn as you mature spiritually. The relationship with God starts with baby faith, where God is doing everything for you and reassuring you of His love all the time. It grows into teenage faith. He's always there for you and tells you He loves you. Then there is a time to grow up and go into the world and do what you were sent to the world to accomplish. For a season, it may seem that He's not there. It will require patience. So you have to remember how God was there all the times before. You may hear negative voices that say, "You can't do it. It's too big for you." God says, "Trust Me."

To have patience, you need to know that He is able, that He loves you, that He has made promises to you (I will never leave you or forsake you).

While you're patient, God builds spiritual muscle in you. The Word says, "Knowing this, that the trying of your faith worketh patience. But let patience have her perfect work, that ye may be perfect and entire, wanting nothing" (James 1:3–4, KJV).

As you're being patient, God will intervene to give you the desire of your heart in one of three ways.

1. He shows or tells you how to make it.
2. He draws a blessing to you.
3. He tells you where to go get it.

One of the fine young men who attended one of my Vertical Leap Seminars (see page i for information on how you can attend) told the following story of going from hope to a thing. See if you can identify the steps he took and the method of intervention God used in his life.

"For a long time I drove a Biscayne, which is like a cheap version of a Belair. It looked like a boat on wheels and handled that way, too. People honked at me at lights and yelled, 'Get that hunk of junk out of the way.' I wanted a truck. So I remembered what God had done for me in the past. Once He healed me from a dislocated shoulder while waiting in the emergency room for treatment. My hope turned into belief as I remembered what God did. Then I started to take action. I called used car lots and told them what I wanted and left my name and phone number. Then I had to have some patience. Finally, I got a call back about a truck with all the things I asked God for. So I got my truck."

Algebraic Formula for Hope to a Thing

Here's another way of looking at how to turn the invisible into the visible. It's found in Mark 11:22–25, where Jesus gives a formula for bringing about a miracle.

"And Jesus answering saith unto them, Have *faith* in God. For verily I say unto you, that whosoever shall *say* unto this mountain, Be thou removed and be thou cast into the sea; and shall not *doubt* in his heart, but shall *believe* that those things which he saith shall come to pass; he shall have whatsoever he saith. Therefore I say unto you, What things soever ye desire, when ye *pray*, believe that ye receive them, and ye shall have them. And when ye stand praying, *forgive*, if ye have aught against any . . ." (Mark 11:22–25, KJV, italics added for words used in the formula below).

I believe principles can be mathematically proven; therefore, I've turned this passage into an algebraic equation. Here's the formula, first in words, and then in symbols.

Pray in Faith times *Say* (minus *Doubt* plus *Belief*) times *Forgiveness* = *Things*

$$Pf \bullet S(-D+B)Fg = \text{Things}$$

Now let's put numerical values to these concepts.

$$10 \times 5 \, (-1 +9) \, 1 = 400$$

In the equation above, numbers were assigned capriciously, but it's important to see that forgiveness was not at zero. If forgiveness becomes unforgiveness, it would become zero. For example:

$$10 \times 5 \, (-1 +9) \, 0 = 0$$

You pray, talk, and believe, but if you have unforgiveness, it becomes a bottleneck that completely blocks your efforts, and there is zero throughput.

Now let's go through each of the factors of the equation and explain them.

Pray in faith. (See Matthew 6:5–15.) Communicate on the inside with God. Pray without ceasing right NOW. (See Ephesians 6:18.) "In faith," talks about believing/trusting what God is showing you, which is seen as a hope, a vision, or an idea. Remember, faith will cause action. Faith is your belief in motion.

Say. You need to tell your vision. There is always somebody prepared to bless you with favor in the thing God has called you to. Someone is waiting to hear the word God tells you to speak. They will say, "I don't know what it is about that person, but I like him. I want to bless him." People are attracted when you believe in what you're talking about. Belief is magnetic in attracting favor.

Forgive. You can't enter into a relationship with Jesus when you've got presuppositions based on the wrongs other people have done to you. The blessings of God are like having access to fresh water from an artesian well. God pours this fresh water into your jug. But what if you keep a dead rat in your jug? All your water tastes like dead rats. That dead rat is unforgiveness that you harbor from your past—your past hurts and failed relationships, prejudices, presuppositions, people taking advantage of you. You judge new people by past hurts. You contaminate and sabotage the new by your unforgiven past. Not only do you have to forgive others, but you have to forgive yourself. You will have failure-causing habits in your life until you get rid of the dead rats. Remember, your decision to forgive will determine the quality of your blessing—zero, thirty, sixty, a hundredfold return (Matt. 13:23).

"Forgive, if you have aught against any: that your Father also which is in heaven may forgive you your trespasses. But if ye do not forgive, neither will your Father which is in heaven forgive your trespasses" (Mark 11:25–26, KJV).

So in Mark 11:22–25 Jesus tells us how to go from the invisible to the visible and how to keep from hindering God's flow of blessing in our lives. Forgiveness is a major, major issue in going from hope to a thing.

In this next section you'll learn how to defeat attacks from the invisible realm that try to keep you from your blessing in the visible realm.

Ganged Up on in the Spiritual Dimension

Have you ever noticed how much a cold can control you? It's such a minor thing, but it can keep you from working toward your vision from God for a week or more.

What about when you are angry with someone? Your mind may be consumed with how you were wronged. Your creative energy is sapped away with these useless thoughts.

Have you ever experienced depression? You can almost audibly hear voices telling you that your situation is hopeless and that you should give up and stop trying.

Do these situations just happen randomly as a "part of life"? I don't think so. Many of them are the result of attacks from satanic forces in the spirit dimension. Think for a moment about what satanic strategies seem to be used against you right now.

To win the battle, we need to be aware of the hierarchy of dimensions. The physical world has three dimensions. The first dimension is length (a straight line). The second contains both length and width. The third dimension has length, width, and depth.

The fourth, and higher, dimension cannot be measured or weighed. In physics, the fourth dimension would be time, but for our purposes I will call the fourth dimension the spiritual realm.

The spirit realm contains the spirit side of man, his heart, and mind. It is also the place where Satan and his demons dwell.

Above all dimensions is eternity, where God dwells. The law of dimensions says that all lesser dimensions are contained in higher dimensions.

Hierarchy of Dimensions

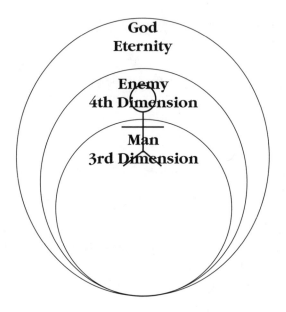

Satanic forces in the spirit dimension seek to rule the third dimension (or physical realm) by controlling your head and your heart. They do not manifest in physical bodies, but they attack your will power through *vain imagining, negative memories, destructive emotions, and worldly intellect.*

Remember, your state of mind in the spirit realm will affect the condition of your body in the physical realm, so these spirit dimension attacks can also produce headaches, colds, and other illnesses.

"For we are not fighting against people made of flesh and blood, but against persons without bodies—the evil rulers of the unseen world, those mighty satanic beings and great evil princes of darkness who rule this world; and against huge numbers of wicked spirits in the spirit world" (Eph. 6:12, TLB). When you are isolated and alone, you get ganged up on by these evil spirit forces.

The enemy wants to sever our link with God as he did with Adam and Eve. He tries to keep us from being vessels of productivity for God's will so that he can use us for his own purposes in the third dimension. He'll corrupt your presuppositions, beliefs, and potential to keep you from trusting God. He'll also make you think you're too busy with your problems to worship God for nourishment and power.

A quick way that Satan can disconnect us from God is to get us to disobey God, even if it's just in a small way. No matter how small our disobedience is, it's sin. We don't have to murder anybody, just disobey God and obey the devil. When I disobey God I lose my peace—I'm disconnected.

If God is not filling you and leading you, then the enemy is. Satan will offer you things of the earth. That's what he offered Jesus. (See Luke 4:1–13.) We have to go before God and ask, "Am I off the right path?" You know you're off the right path when you're putting something before God. It becomes idolatrous. Abraham faced this temptation with his son, Isaac. His son was not God, and if he had put his son in God's place he would have been defeated.

God is jealous in guarding His relationship of bonding with us because it's the only chance you and I have against the demons. They're smarter than us. They've been around longer than you and me.

Seeking Power in the Third Dimension

We have to look for our power from the spirit dimension above us, not the worldly dimension below. If I look for power in the worldly dimension, I'll begin to cannibalize you. And when I dry you up and run you away because I'm hanging on to you so tight, I'll go to somebody else. Nobody can satisfy my emptiness because they're not God. There is not enough of you in the physical realm to satisfy my need in the spiritual.

That's how we ruin relationships. People see when you're a taker. They see you coming and they run. Remember, God's nature is to give. If you're no longer giving and always needing to take, you need to get reconnected to God, the Source.

How to Win

How do I get power over all of these legions of demons? Staying connected with your Source (see principle #2), because "greater is he that is in you, than he that is in the world" (1 John 4:4, KJV). God is so dimensionally great that one of Him is greater than multitudes of these demons. Remember the principle: out of the greater flows the lesser? According to that principle, who made Lucifer? God did.

"For by him were all things created, that are in

heaven and that are in earth, visible and invisible, whether they be thrones, or dominions, or principalities, or powers: all things were created by him, and for him" (Col. 1:16, KJV).

Principalities only exist because God allows them to. That means the Lord could take the devil out any time He wants to.

In the Book of Revelation, it wasn't a major angel that cast the devil into the bottomless pit. It was an unnamed angel. (See Revelation 20:1–3.) When you're connected with God, you can defeat the devil, even if you're an unnamed angel or an ordinary Spirit-filled Christian.

Paul wrote: "It is true that I am an ordinary, weak human being, but I don't use human plans and methods to win my battles. I use God's mighty weapons, not those made by men, to knock down the devil's strongholds. These weapons can break down every proud argument against God and every wall that can be built to keep men from finding him" (2 Cor. 10:3–5, TLB).

How *Not* to Fight in the Spirit Realm

You might think that I'm telling you how to fight the devil. I am, but our battle is not with him directly. Our battle is to stay connected to our power Source by staying in the worship and praise of God. Just keep your mind stayed on Me, He said (Isa. 26:3).

You don't want to give your attention to these demonic powers because anything you give attention to, its spirit comes to live in you. Many people say, "I'm putting the devil under my feet." They're always talking devil, devil, devil. Jesus didn't even speak to the devils. He told them to shut up. (See Mark 1:25.)

You know how a wayward child causes you to lose focus on other things because you spend so much time on them. It's the same effect when you focus on Satan to the exclusion of God. We spend a lot of time on the devil, when we should be spending time with God. Jesus already defeated the devil. God called us to fight the good fight of faith (1 Tim. 6:12). The battle is the Lord's to fight (1 Sam. 17:47). It is no longer you. It is Christ that lives in you (Gal. 2:20).

Our effort is to put on the armor of God. "Last of all I want to remind you that your strength must come from the Lord's mighty power within you. Put on all of God's armor so that you will be able to stand safe against all strategies and tricks of Satan. For we are not fighting against people made of flesh and blood, but against persons without bodies—the evil rulers of the unseen world, those mighty satanic beings and great evil princes of darkness who rule this world; and against huge numbers of wicked spirits in the spirit world" (Eph. 6:10–12, TLB).

Summary

Let's see how our hope-to-a-thing steps, the algebraic formula, and the battle in the spirit dimension all tie together.

As you take the steps from hope to belief to faith to a thing, you are constantly touchstoning. As you remember God's goodness through worship and praise, you reinforce your connection with Him. The algebraic formula reminds us to take out things that would sever the connection—doubt and unforgiveness. The spirit dimension is where we are living out the steps and the formula. Satan attacks us there, but God fights for us when we are connected with Him.

There's a big difference between the way a Christian births a vision, as opposed to someone who doesn't have the benefit of a connection with God. That's why Vertical Leap is about spiritual principles. It's not about what I can do. It's about what God does through me.

The next spiritual principle looks at the advantage of spiritual business practices over nonspiritual business practices. Get ready to create—don't just trade.

APPLICATION QUESTIONS

1. A touchstone is a time that God moved on your behalf. You build up your faith by remembering this touchstone. What is a touchstone in your life?

   _____

   _____

2. Patience builds spiritual muscle. In what area of your life are you practicing patience?

   _____

3. You need to tell your visions because God has prepared somebody to bless you in it. What's one way God has prompted you to tell about your vision? (Don't forget about mass media.)

_____

_____

4. Unforgiveness sabotages our efforts to go from hope to a thing. Do you need to forgive someone? Do you need to forgive yourself?

_____

_____

5. Do you ever focus so much on defeating Satan that you take your eyes off God? How can you avoid this?

_____

_____

Chapter 6

Principle #4
Create; Don't Just Trade

We are constantly engaging in commerce, whether we are aware of it or not. Some of us do it very successfully and some do it very poorly, but we'd better understand the system of commerce if we intend to succeed in it.

The principle of commerce is this: Within my own self I am incomplete; therefore, I must reach outside of my borders to be made whole. Commerce occurs in much more than business. It also takes place in all of our relationships.

People need other people to make them complete. When you marry or establish friendships, you're engaging in commerce. I reach out beyond my borders and bring in resources that will make me more complete—companionship or pleasure, for example. I give something to get something.

As children of God, we haven't been trained in the systems of commerce. We just go and do things. He/she looked good so we got married. That looked like a good business idea, so we signed the contract. When it doesn't work, our hearts are broken.

Commerce occurs in one of three ways—*war, barter and trade, or creativity.* Understanding what kind of commerce you are engaging in will help you be much more successful in interacting with the people around you.

Method of Commerce #1: War

The most rudimentary type of commerce is war. I'm bigger and stronger than you, and I want what you've got, so I take it from you. In Scripture this was the primary process by which people got a bigger piece of the pie. They gathered a big army, stormed the gates, enslaved the people, took what they wanted, and gave it to their own. That was legitimate commerce back then.

The problem with commerce by war is that you make enemies and create saboteurs. When you overpower me and take my things, I don't like you. If you ever close your eyes, I'm going to pay you back. We see this in the Middle East. Sabotage is constantly occurring. The Palestinians were subdued by war so they fight back. In the United States the gang communities do commerce by war. You shot my homey; I'm going to shoot you.

The problem with commerce by war for Christians is that the Holy Spirit in you will not allow you to do evil. The nature of the Spirit is love. Christians can't go out and shoot someone and take their car or belongings.

But there are other people out there who are mean and evil and don't care. You can't get ugly enough for what the devil has as ugly. They don't care what happens to you as long as they get what they want.

Even if Christians won't go out and shoot people for material gain, many of us do commerce by war in relationships. Some men use bullying and threats of violence to get their way. Women are intimidated into submission, but submission doesn't bring about love and trust. Those relationships end with divorce and a woman ready to take revenge however she can.

War is an inferior method of commerce.

Method of Commerce #2: Barter and Trade

This is a form of commerce that is appropriate to practice at times, but it does have shortcomings. In barter and trade, you take an excess commodity from within your borders and give it to someone else in exchange for something you lack.

A simple transaction would work this way. You want to make pancakes, and you have two dozen eggs but no flour. So you go to your neighbor and offer him one dozen eggs for a bag of flour. If your neighbor has extra flour and needs eggs, then you make a trade.

Imbalance of Trade. One problem with barter and trade commerce is that there will always be one side with an imbalance of trade. We see that with Japan and the United States. We buy many more things from Japan than they buy from us. Why? Because we want the things they have.

Another kind of imbalance occurs when the exchanged goods are not of equal value. For example, you and I agree to trade one pound of wheat for one pound of cotton. But you cheat and take some of the wheat you owe me and give it to someone else. So when I give you a pound of cotton, you only have half a pound of wheat to give me.

Imbalance of trade in relationships can make you do things you don't want to do. Imagine you're a single woman on a date with a man. He gives you gold, jewelry, and a mink coat, and you accept them. That night he takes you to your door and says, "Pucker up. I want a kiss." Are you going to kiss him? Yes. You've lost power by receiving a gift that you could not return in equal measure. That's how the devil does it. He puts people in bondage by giving them gifts they do not have the ability to repay. That's why the Bible says the borrower is the servant of the lender. (See Proverbs 22:7.) You should only have the debt of love (Rom. 13:8).

In operating businesses, I see the power of being the lender. For example, if a salesman gives a gift to a buyer, the buyer will feel indebted. That's good for the salesman, however, the buyer loses power. Good buyers don't accept gifts that will compromise their power.

Offense and Defense. Imbalance in trade causes one party to be on offense, and the other to be on defense. Offense says you need me more than I need you. Defense says I recognize that you've got the ball, and I need to get it from you.

The most critical point of success or failure in commerce is the relational attitude you assume with others. When are you on offense and when are you on defense? The location, point in time, and people involved will determine whether you are offense or defense.

Say you come to my office to sell me a product, and tons of other salespeople selling the same product are already in my lobby. In this situation some salespeople effort to be on offense when they are really on defense. They may falsely exaggerate their position, which will define how they treat me. They may come in arrogantly without giving proper respect.

In a home, the roles of offense and defense are often determined by which room of the house you're in. The man usually has an office or garage that's his, and someone else can't go in there and start moving stuff. Often, the woman is in charge of the rest of the house. In each case, respect toward the offense is expected for harmony and peace.

You need to know what you're in charge of and what you're not. If you try to be in charge everywhere, you're going to have problems.

What if your boss comes to your house and the rule at your house is to take off your shoes, but he doesn't do it? He just walks right in with his shoes on, opens the refrigerator, and helps himself. He is not respecting that you have the offense at your house. If he's smart, he'll know he's in charge at the office, but he's on defense at your home.

Many of us fail because we are so caught up in pride that we won't admit when we are on defense, and we try to be on offense in all situations. We don't take the time to think, "Do they need me more than I need them or the other way around?" Can you think of a time when you chose the right stance and were successful? How about a time when you chose the wrong stance and failed? How could you have handled that situation differently?

Barter and Trade by Godly Principles. We don't like to be on defense, but when you see "servant" or "submission" in God's Word, you see the "greatest among you" (Matt. 23:11, KJV). The greatest one among you will outserve the other. We read in 1 Corinthians 13 that you can do great things, but if God's love (charity) isn't working through you, you have nothing. It is a waste of your energy and time. Everything points to servanthood.

In Matthew 5 Jesus gives conditions by which we can succeed, even when we're on defense. Be forewarned, however, they are counter to our human logic.

Jesus said if you're slapped on one cheek, offer the other one, too (Matt. 5:39). If you've ever been in a fistfight, you know how much that would grate against your instincts.

Then Jesus said that if you get sued in court and they demand you give up your coat, then give them your shirt, too (Matt. 5:40). If you had a lawyer today give you that kind of advice, you'd fire him, right?

In Jesus' day the Roman military could demand you carry their gear for a mile. Jesus said, "Why don't you carry it two miles for them" (Matt. 5:41)?

You succeed by giving more than is required of you. That is what God is saying to Christians in this barter and trade relationship. You have the capacity to outlast in love and gain offense through giving where others can't hang. You can give and give until eventually others can't live without you.

Restaurants that really succeed give you more than you could ever eat. We've learned this lesson from giving out the towels at our resort. We thought at first we gave people enough towels, but then we learned that we have to give in abundance.

Most of us give a little until it starts working and then we say, "I'm not going to give any more, you old, greedy thing," and you don't make it to the fullness. But remember, you give because it is God's nature in you to give. You don't give seeking a return.

Your giving is directed by the Lord. We're not to give unless He directs us to do so.

If you give and give and never get a penny back, don't be hostile because you gave it to the Lord. If you're carrying a bad attitude, you weren't giving as unto the Lord. You were doing commerce, and you just got beat out of a deal.

Reasons for Failure in Barter and Trade. When you're conducting commerce by barter and trade, you will experience some failures. We tend to blame others, but the blame rests with us 97 percent of the time. Here are the three reasons for failure I've observed from my years of counseling.

1. Ignorance. I didn't know our commerce wasn't working. People get divorces out of ignorance. Most of the time the relationship didn't have to go bad, but one of the parties didn't realize that they had offended their mate so deeply. There was a lack of good communication. Eighty-seven percent of the reason commerce fails is because of lack of proper communication. We presuppose someone is out to get us. Friendships are destroyed because one party is hurt, and they assume the other person did it on purpose. The truth is, the other person just went unconscious for a moment and acted without thinking.

2. Stupidity. Stupidity accounts for 10 percent of the reason commerce fails. Stupidity is entering into a commerce relationship with a party who can't deliver what you want. You get frustrated, but it's your fault. You should have communicated what you desired and verified that they could deliver (more on this in principle #7). Now you're disappointed that the drunk you married won't become a deacon at the church. He's not able. It's like asking a paraplegic to run a mile in 3:39. He doesn't have the capacity to do it.

3. Sabotage. Most people blame sabotage as the number 1 reason for why commerce fails. "The other person was out to get me." But that's only 3 percent of the time. Most people are not clear-cut evil, just trying to destroy others. Most people want a win-win relationship. They don't want to take, nor do they want to be taken. Sabotage happens when the other person has drawn first blood or you have a presupposition that this is a dog-eat-dog environment and I'd better protect myself.

Barter and trade is an imperfect method of commerce, but there is a type of commerce Christians can use that is perfect. It's called creativity.

Method of Commerce #3: Creativity

Creativity means to produce something where there is nothing. This is where you and I as Christians excel.

There are men who don't have the ability or the knowledge to preach, but they have thousands who listen to them. It's because they take the time to sit before God's face, and God blesses them with a creative anointing.

The best known Bible example of God giving creativity would be Moses. God used him to save Israel from slavery and creatively sustained Israel for forty years in the desert (see Exodus).

Creativity doesn't come by power or might. Don't bother to tell God, "I've got all these degrees" or "I never finished high school." God doesn't care about that.

It's no longer in the physical. It's being governed by the spiritual. If you think about it, you have probably experienced a creative idea from God. Were you ever stumped by a problem and asked God for help? Two hours later a creative, workable solution popped into your brain. You wondered, "Where did that come from?" It's God's creativity working in you.

Modern science actually helps us to see creative power. When science tried to understand the difference between elements, they put atoms under a microscope with a light in order to observe them. They observed that atoms are made up of protons, neutrons, and electrons. The number and combination of these subatomic particles determine the difference between all material things (hydrogen and gold, pork and cotton, steel, wool, beef, and so on).

However, scientists were surprised to discover that the electrons got so excited from being under the microscope's light that they left their base orbits and became free electrons. These free electrons could join with new atom particles, thus changing the base nature of that to which it had joined (*God and the New Physics* by Paul Davies, Simon and Schuster, New York, 1983).

The key discovery was that light caused change. Jesus says, "I am the light of the world" (John 8:12, KJV). So He is the ultimate change agent. Jesus is the light and the light changes things.

In our world, there is no lack of things to be changed. Our atmosphere is full of atoms. Dirt is everywhere. There are all kinds of atoms. They just need to be rearranged into the things we need. So when Jesus needed to feed the multitude, the material was already there. All He had to do was speak His Word. His word is light, and the matter changed according to His will. Bread and fish came into existence where there was none before.

We can't just speak our words and expect things to change. Jesus is the *pure* light of the Word. So when you speak exactly what God said when He says it, things will change. God's Word spoken through you will cause molecules to change. He "calleth those things which be not as though they were" (Rom. 4:17, KJV). The challenge is, Can we get the purity of God's Word flowing through us? Or will we continue to allow our pasts to contaminate it?

When Jesus needed a young donkey for His entry into Jerusalem, He told His disciples to go into town where they would find the animal and bring it to Him. When they were questioned, Jesus told them to say, "The Lord hath need of him" (Luke 19:31, KJV). When they said exactly what Jesus told them to say, a change occurred in the thinking of the men who possessed the colt. They let the disciples take the colt. The disciples received favor.

Jesus was demonstrating that when we are in fellowship with Him and speak the purity of His words at the time He tells us to, He will cause things to change that we could not change ourselves. Jesus *is* the light, and light changes things.

Remember, however, sacrifice precedes blessing. That means you're going to have to spend time being bonded to Him. That's why there's a whole chapter in this book about bonding with your source. You can read about people like Kathryn Kuhlman who saw great miracles of healing. They spent enormous amounts of time in the worship and praise of God. Most of us want to be giants in the spirit, but we don't want to give up anything to get there. We're not disciplined.

Remember I shared my testimony earlier in this book how I was bankrupt and how the pain of this condition drove me to bond with God. Out of that bonding through suffering and sacrifice came a successful multimillion-dollar business, a national ministry, and the book you are now reading.

Summary

The point of studying kingdom commerce is to realize that we as Christians have a great advantage in this area. In barter and trade we have a source to help us give even when others can't give back. We also have the ability to win even when we're on defense. *In creativity we can turn to God for dreams, visions, and ideas that we never could have on our own;* plus, He gives us favor through worship and trusting Him.

In chapter 2 I told you how important it is to

stay conscious. In the next chapter we'll go into depth about how staying conscious can help us to overcome negative things that have been programmed into our subconscious minds. Every person in the world needs to understand how their subconscious mind works, so don't put this book down now. Keep reading to learn how to reprogram your subconscious mind so that you can give birth to God's dreams for you.

APPLICATION QUESTIONS

1. In any situation, you must decide whether you have the offensive or defensive position. What gives you the confidence to accept to be on defense rather than insist to be on offense? (See Matthew 5:39–41.)

2. Creativity is spiritual, not physical. Have you ever asked God to help you solve a problem with a creative idea? What problem can He help you with now?

3. Do you believe Jesus can transform matter from one substance to another by His Word? How do you think you would need to change in order to have the purity of God's Word flow through you?

Chapter 7

Principle #5
Reprogram Your
Subconscious Mind

Did you know your brain has the capacity to process more than one hundred million bytes of information per second? The Bible from Genesis to Revelation only contains five million bytes of information. So you have the capacity to process the entire Bible over twenty times per second.

The *Encyclopedia Britannica* contains about 43.7 million bytes of information. Your brain has the capacity to process all the knowledge of the *Encyclopedia Britannica* more than two times per second.

If you took all the knowledge ever known to man and downloaded it onto the hard drive of your brain, you would have 75 percent of your storage capacity still available.

Social scientists say the brain has no limitations. It is a muscle that continues to develop and grow. You don't have to exchange it for the latest hardware update.

So when you and I use words like "I can't" or "It's impossible" we're talking as fools because reality is that we are geniuses whose minds have been poorly programmed.

You may believe you are clumsy or stupid or ugly or shy or rude. Who told you so? Is that reality? Or did it come from a poor programmer at a time when you weren't mature enough to see the truth?

In this chapter, we are not going to judge and blame. But we are going to take a look at some of those areas we have not been growing through and recognize that we can, as adults, choose not to be afraid and go back to reprogram bad files.

Your Brain Determines Reality

We understand the capacity of the brain, so the question is, Why are we living beneath our potential?

Your brain creates your reality, but the brain can be affected by drugs, stress, pain, anger, and so on. For example, if you were color blind, under the influence of drugs you might possibly see colors. The point I want to make is that the reality perceived by your brain can be altered.

The scientific term for how man acquires knowledge is *epistemology*. The brain does not get information about the outside world directly. Its three pounds of flesh is shielded from the world by a bony prison called the cranium. The brain acquires information through four outside sources:

1. Five senses—sight, sound, smell, touch, and taste. The body changes those sensations into chemical stimuli that the brain can process.
2. Reasoning—reorganization of information taken from sensory experiences. If sensory input is inaccurate, reasoning will be inaccurate.
3. Intuition—inner knowing shaped from belief, thoughts, and feelings.
4. Culture/authority—words and modeling from parents, peers, teachers, and others who influence you.

These are the four primary sources that program our brains with reality.

How Words Affect the Brain

When our brains receive impressions, they are expressed as words or thoughts/pictures. When these word pictures are allowed to linger in the mind as thoughts, they shape our character and ultimately the circumstances of the world around us. This can be for good or bad. The more energy, focus, or repetition we give a thought, the more influence it has. "As [a man] thinketh in his heart, so is he" (Prov. 23:7, KJV).

Words are to the mind as gas is to an engine. When the mind is mobilized by words, it can cause the physical body to create or destroy. Voodoo and juju have shown how our minds can affect our physical well-being. You may be under a spell right now. Someone said something to hurt your feelings, and now you have a headache or a cold. It was psychosomatic: the state of the mind affected the condition of the body.

In a dream God showed me the power of words over a person. I dreamed I was attending a class about words, and the teacher told us that the right words were all that were needed to restore a man to wholeness in spirit, soul, and body. As a demonstration, the teacher took the class on a field trip to an old bus station. The people at the station were slumped in their seats, drooped and depressed like wilted flowers. The teacher went to each person, lifted his or her head, and asked if he might sing. Each person nodded in agreement, though with much effort. The teacher then began to sing these words, "Can you let your light shine in my dream? Don't give up on my dream. You can make it if you try." As he gently lifted each head and sang these words, each person would take on new life, like a wilted flower being drenched with water. Words and word perceptions (hostile looks and gestures) had withered those people, and godly words brought them back to life.

When Were You Programmed?

How was your reality programmed? What words entered into your brain and formed your character?

It's important to understand that the most significant period for programming your brain is from 0 to 14 years of age. That's because you are so young and inexperienced that you do not question the input that you receive. So instead of processing the information in your conscious mind, you accept directly into your subconscious. I'll talk more about conscious and subconscious mind in the next chapter. For now, just keep in mind that your childhood perception of reality was placed into your subconscious mind.

Thinking back to your childhood may be painful, but it's important to do it now because it will help you see how to fully release your potential.

We'll look at two age spans in general: zero to seven and eight to fourteen. Within these ranges we'll also look at more specific time periods. (The Life Phases chart I've included on the following page for your reference shows the entire life span for your information.)

Zero to Seven Years

From zero to seven years of age is the most critical period when those files of reality are being shaped. The primary programmer for this period is the parent or person raising the child. So if your parent was going through drugs or relational problems, you, the baby, suffered for it. That is going to have a major role on your ability to grow in the ways that we are going to discuss.

Many of us have parents who were quite young when they had us. Now you have younger sisters or brothers who are much more stable than you are and you ask, "Why are they doing so well when I am doing so poorly?" The answer is that your household had changed by the time your brothers or sisters came along. Your mother or

Life Phases Chart*

Life Phases	Cultural Influences			
	1	2	3	4
0–7	Parent	Sibling	Teacher	
8–14	Teacher	Siblings	Parents	Peers
15–21	Peers	Mate	Teacher	
22–25	Mate	Family	Peers	Job/Boss
28–29	Job/Boss	Family	Mate	
30–37	Job/Boss	Family	Mate	
38–44	Job/Boss	Family	Mate	
45–51	Job/Boss	Comm/church	Mate	
52–58	Comm/church	Job/Boss	Mate	
59–65	Mate	Comm/church	Job	
65	Mate	Comm/church		

Infancy (0–15 mos.): Waking up emperor syndrome.

Early Childhood (1–3 yrs.): Curiosity/afraid to take risk.

Middle Childhood (3–7 yrs.): Discovering differences.

Late Childhood (7–12 yrs.): Consolidating growth gained—feeling inadequate.

Mid-Adolescence (15–18 yrs.): Physical and psychological turmoil. Independence from authority. Trial and error; must learn to accept failure.

Late Adolescence (18–22 yrs.): Parent/child conflict stabilizes. Long for intimacy with others. Key: Responsibility, keeping agreements. Strong sense of self. Sexual intimacy—open, sharing, trusting and honesty.

Young Adult (22–30 yrs.): Mating/Parenting—achieving a clear picture of capacities, limitations for the rest of life. Change jobs, accept responsibility, learning to make decisions.

Adult (30–45 yrs.): Growth and stabilizing. Growth and acceptance of goals. Period of making right choices—stable for the next fifteen years, best performance-cost energy. Increased knowledge in skill and learning—good relationship with parents, marriage. Self-esteem at highest point. Must remember to balance.

Middle Years (45–55 yrs.): Time of transition. How do I live the rest of my life? Take stock—children gone. Self-image concerns.

Late Years (55–65 yrs.): Ailments in bodies, unresolved conflicts. Religion very important. Workmanship, letting the past go. Appreciate beauty.

Old Age (65 and over): Accept death, friends die, seeking to diminish fear of death. Quality of life—cleans up old things, preparing to leave.

*Adapted from: James L. Christian, *Philosophy: The Art of Wondering* (San Francisco, Rinehart Press).

father had become much smarter about how to rear a child. You were the trial model.

The second most important influence from zero to seven is your siblings. Did you get teased a lot by your siblings? Were you called dumb or stupid, teased for having a big forehead or big feet? Still today, you wear your hair a certain way or act a certain way because of what they said.

It's been stated, "Sticks and stones may break my bones, but words will never hurt me." That is so untrue. The broken bones will heal, but the scars that words leave do not heal automatically.

Now let's look at some specific development periods from zero to seven years of age.

Zero to Fifteen Months (Infancy). This is the period when a child learns to trust. During the 1960s, prevailing opinion was that when babies cried you gave them a little attention and then left them in their cribs to cry it out. You don't pamper. You don't spoil the child. That devastated a whole generation of people. Being left to cry to exhaustion caused some to be programmed to believe the world is a cruel, untrustworthy place.

Some social scientists believe that zero to fifteen months is when psychotics are formed. That's because a true psychotic is one whose trust in his environment is so low that he can do horrible things and feel justified.

Many of us were not attended to properly during that period of life. No telling what your parents were going through at that time—divorce, separation, drugs. Psychosis is an extreme reaction, but lack of trust manifests in many other ways. You may wonder why you can't let people get close to you, even though they embrace you and love you and cause you to want to trust. You think the problem is in your nature, when it is in your programming.

Others have an attitude that says, "If I have to abuse you to get my pleasure, so what? If you don't take care of yourself, that's your problem. I've got to take care of me."

Do you wonder how you can be so cold and insensitive? Then ask about your parents' lives when you were an infant. Were you left with a family member, friend, or babysitter who abused you?

One to Three Years (Early Childhood). The one to three period is when you learn how to take risks. This is when you experience reality firsthand for yourself. There are two sides to this: you can learn to fear risk, or you can learn to be reckless.

Let's say for example you and your parents were living in someone else's home. When you went to touch something in that home they needed so desperately to live in, they would tell you, "Don't you touch; sit down; don't move."

Or say you were told to get a glass and you reached up and grabbed a glass and then dropped it. An authority figure takes out their frustration on you: "You clumsy ox! Why don't you watch what you're doing?" You're afraid to reach out for anything now. It was a shock to your system, and the file was launched. "I'm a klutz. I'd better not take risks anymore."

There are many people who have master's degrees and doctor's degrees, but they can't take a risk. You've been a student all your life. You've gone to college and acquired all this education, but when it comes to starting your practice, you can't take a risk.

Now let's look at how you can become pro-grammed to take unreasonable risks. Let's say you grew up in a home where nobody told you what to do. No one took the time to discipline you as a toddler. When you got older you were a latchkey kid. Momma wasn't home or didn't care or was on drugs. Nobody told you when to come home or when go to bed. So now you grow up and you have a relationship and that person asks, "What time are you coming home tonight?" You say, "How dare you? Nobody tells me what to do."

Some people go to Las Vegas and gamble and take crazy risks. You marry them, and they gamble away your rent and you wonder, "What's wrong with him?" Maybe he grew up with so much freedom that now he takes unnecessary risks.

Three to Seven Years (Middle Childhood). From three to seven years is when a child gets a sense of the differences between people, including sexual differences. The child learns what it means to be male or female.

Many men today grow up in a matriarchal envi-ronment, and it really affects their ability to know who they are. What if you're a male growing up in an all-female house? You used to be able to go into the toilet with Momma and the rest of the kids but now Momma won't let you go into the toilet with her while sisters Sally and Susan do. You wonder, "What's wrong with me? Does Momma love them more than me?" Inferiority gets written in the files.

In your home you may have heard the women talking about men as "good-for-nothing dogs" when they thought you were not listening. But you heard and you were writing files about how men can't be trusted and they're dogs and they hurt people. Now you ask, "What kind of a person am I?"

You want to model the one you admire, the one who gave you attention. If Daddy isn't there, who do you want to emulate? Some men grow up wanting to put on lipstick and high heels. Some women emulate the males. Now they are saying, "What's wrong with me?"

What about the single mother who was lonely and got into a relationship? Mom needed somebody to give her some attention, and the walls were paper thin, so you heard the noises and the sounds of the spirit of lust. That spirit could have come to live in you.

Eight to Fourteen Years

The primary files are set between zero and seven years. But between eight to fourteen years, you're still flexible enough that you can be molded. There is an advantage over the zero-to-seven period because the programmer doesn't have to deal with your babyness. The programmer doesn't have to start with the beginning base clay. You're almost complete, however, the programmer can still shape the clay.

Teachers. During these years, the prominence of the primary programmers is re-ordered. Would it surprise you to know that teachers have the most influence? What nature are they placing in our children? The world is really in charge of this period, but the church needs to take it back.

Teachers in school say, "If you have a problem with your momma, come to me." What's the message in that? "If your momma hurt you, come talk to me about it. I'll put her in jail." Can you see how the primary programmer has become the teacher?

That teacher defines whether you're smart or dumb. Your self-esteem is riding on that apple being properly polished for that teacher. "That teacher doesn't like me. That teacher has given me a bad grade. When I look at the teacher, she never gives me eye contact. She never calls on me. What's wrong with me? Why am I always getting overlooked? Why am I always getting kicked to the curb? What's wrong with me? Am I valuable? Is that my reality?"

The problem is that the teacher likely gave you a false reality. Say you failed your math class and the teacher got mad at you. Maybe the teacher did not take the time to find out how much school you missed because you and your momma didn't have a place to live. On the day of the final exam, you didn't even get breakfast. You weren't sure if you would eat lunch. Your clothes didn't look good, so you dressed in somebody else's hand-me-downs. The other kids "dissed" you on the way to school, and then you had to face a math problem. Are you dumb or overwhelmed?

The teacher calls you dumb by giving you a D-, which says to you, "You don't have the stuff to make it in life. Don't worry about going to college. You're not smart enough."

So that teacher's wordless words got into your file. As an adult, when you try to get the job or make the sale, your files say, "They won't choose me. I'm not good enough. I can't compete."

As a child, you didn't realize that the teacher could misjudge you. What was going on in her life? That teacher might have been going through a divorce or teetering at the brink of her own mental stability. How could she lead you when she couldn't even lead herself? And she was responsible for programming you into greatness? How was she supposed to teach you to succeed when she felt like a failure?

Siblings. Just as in the zero to seven stage, siblings are the second most important influence. What do siblings do in this eight-to-fourteen-year span? Generally, they pick on any physical defect they can find. Unfortunately, a lot of us looked weird at this age. We grew into our body features as adults, but we looked weird then.

Your teeth are falling out, and they're crooked. Your legs are too long. Your behind is too big. In your childhood, everybody called you "Forehead"— friends, sisters, and brothers. Years later they say they were only teasing, but your messed up files show that their words affected you.

I don't even know where to start on the issue of puberty. For women, the breasts didn't grow fast enough. All the other girls had them and you didn't. Men, it was a horror going into those communal high school showers. You didn't develop fast enough. People teased you. You wondered, "Am I OK?"

Parents. Parents will be relieved to know that they at least make third on the list of influences at this age. If a parent makes a conscious effort, he or she can counteract the negative programming that can occur at this time. This is an important time for parents to bond with the children. Role modeling is crucial to this period. Someone or thing is mentoring your child—TV, computer games, gang leaders, or you.

So this process of programming continues, with parents, teachers, siblings, and friends all contributing to the files. The immature mind accepts these files indiscriminately, whether they are accurate reflections of reality or not.

If you did not have a relationship with Jesus as a child, the files launched into your brain by the outside world were your only perception of reality. That's why many of us need reprogramming with the truth of God's Word. (See Romans 12:2.)

Reprogramming the Files

How do we reprogram the files in the subconscious mind? I will focus on three areas.

1. Replace a bad habit with a good habit, using the REPOH formula.
2. Shock treatment.
3. God's divine plan.

Replacing a Bad Habit with a Good Habit, Using REPOH

This teaching is one of the most important principles you can gain from this book because creating a good habit is valuable in so many areas. The technique for doing it can be remembered with the acronym REPOH.

What you do *repetitiously* becomes easy.
When it becomes *easy* it will bring pleasure.

When it brings *pleasure*, you will do it often.
What you do *often* will become a *habit*.

You can also remember the steps by saying them like a rap: Repetition, easy—easy, pleasure—pleasure, often—often, habit.

Let's say you were programmed to believe the world is a hostile place. As a result, you have a hard time saying "I love you" to your wife. The new habit you want to create is to say "I love you" to her.

You need to program your conscious mind so that it will override the files in your subconscious mind. This is done by exercising the conscious mind, using REPOH. The key to effectiveness is that you must say the formula aloud, naming your new habit as you do. So when you're saying the formula, you don't ever use the word *it*. This exercise will cause you to think before you speak versus responding subconsciously. The idea is to practice being conscious of every word spoken. You should learn to taste every word. For example:

> As I say, "I love you," saying "I love you" becomes easy.
> As saying "I love you" becomes easy, saying "I love you" becomes a pleasure.
> As saying "I love you" becomes a pleasure, saying "I love you" is done often.
> As saying "I love you" is done often, saying "I love you" becomes a habit.

Repeat the formula over and over until your

conscious choice becomes your new habit of thinking. You have to change your thought process before you can take a new action. If I can change my thoughts, then I can change my feelings, followed by my actions and my attitude. Then my belief will change and form my new potential. My potential will become my new presuppositions (paradigms).

Before you read any further, try putting a good habit you'd like to develop into the formula. Speak it aloud. Speaking is harder when you must think first. I challenge you to try.

By the simple process of no longer using the pronoun *it* in the formula, you are forced to think with your conscious mind. The subconscious doesn't require you to think. It just controls you with old habits created in the past. By speaking the formula in a conscious state, the conscious mind can reprogram data into the subconscious file.

In the past much of the conscious mind was driven by the subconscious mind's data. Now you're going the other way around—the conscious impacting the subconscious.

Your subconscious file is based on the past. Your new file is based on your conscious choices.

We are no longer slaves to reality from the past. We learn to think before we speak or react, which makes the Word of God our driving force instead of our old habits.

Shock Treatment

This is another way for a file to be rewritten for the better. It also tends to hurt. For instance, you tell a child consistently, don't touch the stove. But one time he touched it anyway and got burned. The shock reprogrammed the file. Each time the child goes near the stove, the pain of being burned is brought to his conscious remembrance, so that he no longer decides to touch it.

This is the principle behind some of the boot camps where they send young people who are involved with gangs or making other bad choices. The shock of that environment sometimes helps them to reprogram their files. Adults get shocked, too. Some men get shocked when their wives walk out on them. Some women get shocked when they find their man running around on them. The files get reprogrammed and they start handling relationships differently.

God's Divine Plan

I believe God wants to help us reprogram files that would keep us from fulfilling His plan for us. One way we do this is through prayer and worship. When we enter God's presence through prayer and worship, our spirits are changed into His likeness. Don't ever give up on changing your past programming because with God all things are possible. *Remember, whatever you give your attention to, its spirit will come live in you. Be filled with the Spirit.*

Summary

We've covered a lot of ground with "Reprogram Your Subconscious Mind." We've seen that God has blessed each of us with a brain that has virtually limitless capacity. Then we looked at how our subconscious files limit us according to the programming we received, specifically in our youth. Finally, I gave you three ways to reprogram past files so that you can take that essential Vertical Leap—*from facts to faith to action.*

The next spiritual step is very closely tied to this one. It goes deeper into the interaction between the conscious and subconscious mind to show how the conscious mind can be trained to take control. You don't have to be smart and you don't have to be rich to do what I'm talking about. Just keep reading.

APPLICATION QUESTIONS

1. Words wither people, but words can also bring them back to life. How could you use words to bring life to someone you know?

   _____

   _____

   _____

   _____

2. Were you teased a lot as a child? Do you think that affected how you perceive yourself?

   _____

   _____

3. Do you know who cared for you when you were an infant? Were your needs met lovingly? How do you think that treatment has affected you?

_____

_____

_____

_____

4. Use REPOH (Repetition—Easy—Pleasure—Often—Habit) to start a positive habit.

_____

_____

_____

_____

Chapter 8

Principle #6
Choose Who
Pushes You

Have you ever done something and looked back and said, "I don't understand why I did that. I've always said I would never do something like that, and then I did it. Why?"

A lot of times it was something you disliked in your parents' lives. Your momma was taken advantage of by her boyfriend, and then you get involved with a someone who takes advantage of you. Or your daddy was never there for you and your siblings, then you decide to go play golf instead of watch your own kid's basketball game.

In this chapter I want to go into depth about how to stop doing things that we don't intend to do. The key is understanding the relationship between the conscious and the subconscious mind.

Your Two Minds

Every one of us has a divided mind. The two parts—the conscious and the subconscious—war with each other for prominence. Though they both want control, they are not equally qualified to lead.

The conscious mind is the most qualified leader because it can perform the following four functions:

1. *Recognize.* Find out what is happening in your environment and what God is doing in your life.
2. *Identify.* Determine whether information is true or false, good or bad.
3. *Organize.* Group information for easy identification.
4. *File.* Remember experiences in order to make future decisions.

You can see that the conscious mind is active in processing information and making choices.

In contrast, the subconscious mind makes a poor leader. From the day you were born, it has passively reacted to sensory input. When you were an infant, the subconscious mind worked effectively to ensure your survival. When you were hungry, it told you to holler until you were fed. The subconscious mind made sure your needs were met.

As you grew older, your parents appealed to have your conscious mind override your subconscious desire. This is called becoming mature. For example, when you train children to share and to give, you appeal to the conscious mind. The subconscious mind is not interested in sharing and giving. Its only interest is your bodily pleasure and comfort. Sharing has to be taught. When you hear adults talking "me, my, I" selfishly, they are often talking from the subconscious, which is self-centered.

The subconscious mind is capable of taking in information and does not discriminate whether the information is true or false, good or bad. It will process information based on the programmer's belief. When the subconscious mind hears, "You're lazy," it defines the meaning of lazy by matching lazy to similar subconscious files. It then files that information according to these preprogrammed beliefs. For example, "Uncle Bob was so rich he didn't have to work. He was lazy. Lazy is good." Or "Bill is on drugs and will not work and is lazy. He is an outcast of the family. Lazy is bad."

Battle of the Mind

When you are faced with a decision, the conscious and the subconscious minds start to war. If the conscious does not fight to stay in control, the subconscious mind takes over and pulls up the old past files, which direct you to act out conditioned behavior. These responses are called habits.

Here's a specific example: You grew up in a family where your father abused your mother when there was no food on the table. You say to yourself, "I will never treat my wife like that." Every time you think about what your dad did, you become more and more angry. What happens to that file every time you think about it? Habits form and the file expands. The more I hate it, the more I become like that which I hate because the file takes up more of my mind. The Word of God warns us not to judge (Luke 6:37). *Remember, whatever I give my attention to, its spirit will come live in me.*

You grow up and get married. One day you get laid off on your job. Frustrated, (you're not a Christian) you stop by the bar on the way home and get drunk. The drinks impair the ability of your conscious mind; therefore, you are operating out of your subconscious files. You don't have the ability to recognize, identify, organize, and file. You go home and there is no food on the table. What behavior will be expressed when there's no food on the table and you're unconscious? The subconscious file opens up, and you do what's in the file. You hit. You did exactly what you hated in your father.

When the drinks wear off and you become conscious again, you are sorry you hit her. You allowed your old subconscious file to take control.

Who or What Is Your *Because?*

Ask yourself, *Who is my "because?" Be* means "to exist" and *cause* means "to incite unto action." Whatever pushes you becomes your because. Whatever is your *because* becomes your god.

When we encounter a stimulus, most of us are pushed around by our past programming. That's because we go unconscious and let our subconscious minds rule us. But our actions do not have to be dictated by the stimulus we receive. We can consciously choose what will push us.

In any situation you need to ask, Am I being pushed by good, or not-so-good? If you see that not-so-good from your past is pushing you, then push back! Don't respond to the push from anything other than good. You may need to go back and look at *what pushed* what is pushing you. If not-so-good pushes Person A and in turn Person A pushes you, the domino response will be not-so-good.

How do you recognize what is good? Romans 8:28 says, "And we know that all things work together for good to them that love God, to them who are the called according to his purpose" (KJV). In other words, when God pushes you, it is for your good. You cannot define good by your feelings. What appears to be good could be bad. I can make a lot of money, and it could be bad. There are dope dealers who are rich, but they are miserable.

Keep your mind stayed on God if you want to have good. God's Word says, "Pray without ceasing" (1 Thess. 5:17, KJV). Keep your eyes stayed on Jesus because He is the author and finisher of your faith (Heb. 12:2).

How do I recognize something as God? God is the actual and the actual cannot be in motion. If it moves, it cannot be the alpha and omega. The Bible tells the beginning and the end because God has been there and done that.

The devil doesn't know everything because he hasn't been there yet. Anything that is going somewhere has not yet arrived.

The Vertical Leap means "I will stay conscious and choose who pushes me." Remember, whoever or whatever you allow to push you becomes your god.

What the Bible Says

Have you ever read Paul's discussion in Romans 7 of how he wanted to do good, but he would find himself doing evil instead? In the next few paragraphs we're going to take a fresh look at what Paul said, keeping in mind what we've learned about the conscious and subconscious.

Paul starts by telling what it's like to battle against the subconscious mind without the help of Jesus.

"I felt fine so long as I did not understand what the law really demanded. But when I learned the truth, I realized that I had broken the law and was a sinner, doomed to die" (v. 9, TLB).

When you were unsaved you did not experience guilt—even when you did something wrong—as long as you had filed away that action as good. You didn't know it was wrong because your only feeder of reality came from the subconscious mind. Some people could sleep around as long as they didn't get caught because that's what they heard was good from a parent or peer or culture.

God's law made you aware that you had bad files you thought were good. Now Paul talks about the conscious and subconscious struggle.

"I don't understand myself at all, for I really want to do what is right, but I can't. I do what I don't want to—what I hate" (v. 15, TLB).

Your conscious mind wants to do what is right. But the subconscious mind that is programmed by your past senses, reason, intuition, culture, and authority keeps you from doing it. The carnal man is moved by the subconscious, but the spiritual man is moved by the conscious mind being in alignment with the Holy Spirit.

"I know perfectly well that what I am doing is wrong, and my bad conscience proves that I agree with these laws I am breaking. But I can't help myself, because I'm no longer doing it. It is sin inside me that is stronger than I am that makes me do these evil things" (vv. 16–17, TLB).

The conscious mind knows when you do something wrong, but the sin can overpower the conscious mind. The sin is in that old file in the subconscious. You want to do the right things, but the subconscious file overrules.

"I know I am rotten through and through so far as my old sinful nature is concerned" (v. 18, TLB).

What is rotten through and through? The old files that came from the programmers of the past—parents, teacher, friends, and siblings. (Also how you processed information from your senses, reason, intuition, culture.)

"I love to do God's will so far as my new nature is concerned; but there is something else deep within me, in my lower nature, that is at war with my mind and wins the fight and makes me a slave to the sin that is still within me. In my mind I want to be God's willing servant, but instead I find myself still enslaved to sin" (v. 22ff, TLB).

After Paul got saved, he liked doing good as God defined good. But when he wanted to do right consciously, that subconscious file continued to war against him. He acted out old habits.

"Who will free me from my slavery to this deadly lower nature? *Thank God!* It has been done by Jesus Christ our Lord. He has set me free" (v. 25, TLB, italics added).

"[God] sent his own Son in a human body like ours—except that ours are sinful—and destroyed sin's control over us by giving himself as a sacrifice for our sins. So now we can obey God's laws if we follow after the Holy Spirit and no longer obey the old evil nature within us" (Rom. 8:3–4, TLB).

I want you to see something exciting about what this passage says. Remember how you learned that the most powerful thing that programs our subconscious mind is word perceptions? Here we see that Jesus Christ, who is the perceptible Word, overpowers the bad files that were written by carnal words. He does this for us so that we can live for Him through our conscious minds. It is Jesus, the *rhēmah* word of God, who sets us free.

God Rules in Consciousness

God wants the conscious mind under His influence so that it can override the subconscious mind. The conscious and the subconscious must be in agreement or there will be confusion. "A double minded man is unstable in all his ways" (James 1:8, KJV). Once you believe what God says and you take dominion over the subconscious, it will submit. But it will not submit if you are wishy washy. The conscious mind must believe in its perception of truth without doubting. The subconscious knows if the conscious believes or not, and it cannot be fooled.

So the point of this chapter is this: With the power of God on your side, you have a choice in every situation as to whether you will follow subconscious files of past knowledge or the conscious mind subject to the will of God NOW (zero to five seconds). Ask yourself, *Who pushed me? Was it a file/habit from the past, or was it the Word of God?*

Doesn't it feel good to know you're in charge—that you aren't controlled by someone else's words or actions? Remember, Vertical Leap is about you doing the pushing for a change. In the next chapter you will get the final key to achieving Vertical Leap—system analysis. People who attend Vertical Leap Seminars (see page i for information on how you can attend) love this teaching because it simplifies complex business principles and applies them to relationships and ministry as well as business. Do you want success in all areas of your life? Then keep reading.

APPLICATION QUESTIONS

1. When you are faced with a decision, what percentage of time do you make a conscious choice (as opposed to letting your subconscious files control you)? Do you want to improve that percentage?

   _____

   _____

2. Have your subconscious files been keeping you from success? How?

   _____

   _____

Chapter 9

Principle #7
Analyze Your System

Do you ever wonder why some areas of your life are very successful while the overall picture remains negative? For example, you are the best salesperson at work, but you never get the promotion. Why? Or your husband is a good provider, but he doesn't even buy you a card on Valentine's Day. You have a lot of first-time customers with your business, but they never return.

The secret is to recognize that your life is not made up of unrelated parts. The parts are joined together in systems. If one part of a system is defective, the whole system is crippled. If a crippled system is not repaired, it will lead to other systems failing.

In this chapter, I will show you how to create

and maintain successful systems in your life—both business systems and personal systems.

System Defined

For our purposes, a system is defined as anything with more than one moving part. Do I have more than one moving part? Yes, so I qualify as a system. So if I get into a marriage and bond with someone else who moves, is our marriage a system? Yes. The principle of systems can be applicable to any area of life.

We're going to talk about systems from a business perspective, but I will be continually reminding you that the principles are applicable to your personal life as well.

Dr. Demings and Japan

Any discussion of systems must begin with Dr. W. Edwards Demings (1900–1993), American statistician and quality control expert, and the work he did in Japan after World War II.

After Japan was defeated, their war powers were taken from them. This had the potential to cause an economic crisis because Japan has few natural resources, and in the past they met their needs through commerce by war with their neighboring countries.

The United States and some allied nations began helping Japan start businesses. But Japan didn't have a knowledge for business because their knowledge was for war. Things "made in Japan" had been laughed at for many years because of their poor quality.

So the United States sent Dr. Demings to Japan to improve the quality of their systems. What he did was simple but so revolutionary that it has affected business ever since. He said, "Let's not put our quality control at the end of the line. Let's fix it from the beginning of the line, so it won't be bad at the end of the line."

The waste factor is tremendous when quality control is at the end. Let's say I manufacture cookies. I needed milk for my recipe, but I bought the milk in a hurry. I didn't check to see when I needed the milk. I just bought it and put it in the warehouse. Then when I put the milk into the batter, I discovered it was bad.

How did that affect the rest of my system? It affected the sugar, the flour, the bakers, the equipment, and the environment. I wasted time and space and labor and the other product in the batter. If I had practiced quality control in the beginning I would not have had to say I'm sorry in the end.

Dr. Demings called his system SPC—statistical process control. SPC means monitoring systems proactively by establishing acceptable ranges of performance variance. The goal is to have a total quality system. He applied SPC to everything in manufacturing—people, product, equipment, and environment. SPC is a very powerful principle that you can apply to choice-making throughout life.

The Japanese listened to Dr. Demings and did research and development to improve their production. Everywhere they went they took notes about systems and their performance. They took the best of what existed and learned from it so they would not repeat the errors other people made.

As a result, the Japanese began to rival the American car industry. The Japanese came in with product that would go for years and years.

On the other hand, Americans got in such a hurry to produce cars that they didn't properly check for quality beforehand. You would buy a car and the doors would rattle, Yes, you could take it back, and they would fix it. But that is quality control at the end of the line.

Remember how there were mechanics at every gas station? They were there to fix the American-made cars. But if they had been built right at first, they wouldn't have needed fixing. Gas stations made much of their revenue in repair. Obsolescence was built into the product. American-made cars had a short life span.

If we as a nation hadn't relearned quality control, we would have been devastated.

System Variance

In order to practice SPC you must measure whether the system is operating in acceptable levels of variance.

Any working system has a range of variance. If they put a heart monitor on you and you have a straight line, you're dead. Your system is not working. There will be peaks and troughs in any living system. However, acceptable levels of variance should be determined before developing a system.

In a relationship, I have to watch you enough so that I know the ranges of your attitude. I might see you low here, but you have the potential to go extremely high there. So I have to ask, "How much low can I accept and still achieve a quality relationship?" Once you define your accepted range of variance, you can begin to establish relationships.

We want to set acceptable ranges of variance, but our range should continually get smaller and smaller. We must continually examine our measurements of the system and seek to reduce the level of variance. Constant improvement should be a goal for all systems.

Once we define acceptable ranges of variance, we recognize that every system will have times when things go outside acceptable ranges of variance—in other words, a breakdown. Whenever a system breaks down there is an attack against that system, and it's important for you to find the bottleneck/area of constraint.

The key to correcting a system is never to major on the minors. The minors will come into line when you major on the majors. After you get the principalities in high places under control, the little demonic forces will come in line.

Let's look at this principle in terms of a relationship. So your mate can't stand the way you walk and talk and a bunch of other little things. These little things used to be in the range of acceptable variance. But two weeks ago you came home late smelling like another woman, and now she doesn't like anything about you. Major on the majors and the minors will fall in line.

Four Steps for Good Production

So we recognize that all of us are setting up systems in our lives. First of all, we set up our personal systems. Some of us also have business systems, production systems, mechanical systems, and so on. To set up a system that will succeed according to SPC, you have to take four steps.

As you read through the following pages, refer to the diagram to help you see how the entire system works together.

System Using Statistical Process Control

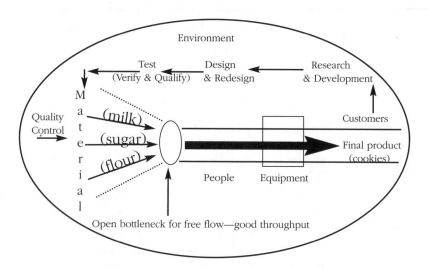

Step #1: Research and Development. Who is my customer; what do they want? A system is driven by a customer. If you don't clearly identify your customer, you don't have a system. The purpose of research and development is to understand the customer.

In a marriage, the wife is the customer of the husband (and vice versa). In the work place, the employer is the customer of the employee. In spiritual life, God is the customer for all of us!

Your good is going to be defined by your customer. You can think you're doing the best job in the world, but if your customer is not pleased, you will go out of business. You must know the likes and dislikes of your customer through careful research. Be careful not to make the common mistake of believing the customer wants what you want or like.

If you're my customer and you don't like what I'm doing, don't lie to me and say it's OK. Tell me you don't like it because I want to stay in business. If you hate the product I produce, and I make a whole lot of this stuff, I'm in trouble. You will be unhappy, which will threaten the life of my system.

If my customer has a need and I tell him, "I can't, impossible," he's going to look for somebody who says, "I will." So if I want to keep him in my system, I had better find out how I can deliver what he wants.

Many people need their jobs desperately, but they disrespect their supervisors, who are their customers. No wonder those employees get passed over for promotions, but the employees may call it prejudice. No, those employees were unconscious. They thought they were in charge when they should have assumed a servant attitude on defense.

If you want to stay employed, give the boss what he wants. If you want a raise, give her more than what she requires of you. You say, "Look at those people, trying to brown-nose the boss, working all those hours." But you may have such an attitude of "I ain't going to give," and that's why you don't have. Christians are to outgive the world.

The life of your system depends on having happy customers. For every one of us, God is our customer. God uses words like, "Obey Me. I'm jealous. Worship." He's asking for extravagant respect—that you would submit your logic and reality to His own.

So to move into this Vertical Leap outside of the three-dimensional realm we have to give our customer what He wants because blessing comes through obedience. To give our Customer what He wants, we must know Him and desire to serve Him with exaggerated respect.

Step #2: Design and Redesign. After I've done my research and development, I'm ready to produce a model or sample of what I believe to be the desire of my customer. The knowledge learned from research and development will guide me in the shaping of this model, which when completed will be offered to my customer for critical review of likes and dislikes. This is a learning period, to be documented for establishing future standard operating procedures (SOP).

Innovation and change is built into systems. The second law of thermodynamics states that systems left to themselves move from order to disorder (entropy). Systems that go unmonitored are doomed for failure. You cannot live in the success of the past. Ask yourself, *How must I adjust to change? How am I able to be a better supplier to my customer?* Redesigning is a constant process because the customer is always changing. Those who succeed will frequently monitor their systems for needed redesign.

Step #3: Testing. The next step in good production is to test. I've been with Fortune 500 companies doing packaging for more than thirty years, and I've never seen them do a nationwide introduction to any new product without first sample market testing. They will do a small-scale test first. Even if they think they know what their customer wants, they aren't going to invest a whole lot of energy, money, or equipment into it until they are sure.

Market testing is a lot better than investing millions in start-up costs and then having to scrap the whole product. They limit their losses by gaining knowledge in the least expensive ways possible.

Many of us don't like this. We start up our systems without counting the cost (businesses, relationships, and so on. (See Luke 14:28.) Then we go out of business. We didn't do research and development, design and redesign, or test our product, so we had no clue as to whether our customers really liked or would buy our product.

Two of the most important words in testing a healthy system are *verify* and *qualify*. Verify means that before I add anything to my system—people, equipment, material, or environment—I'm going to verify that it is *able to perform the task at hand.*

For example, I need a new car that will run consistently at seventy-five miles per hour so I can get to work on time. I've just looked at one of these gorgeous kit cars that you put together yourself, but it only has the capacity to go sixty miles per hour consistently. But it's beautiful. Will I buy that car? No, because it's not able to do the job.

Verifying really applies to relationships. How many people get into relationships and they know that person is an alcoholic or drug addict? They know they can't change him, and yet they go unconscious and try to make it work. Why don't those relationships work? They didn't verify that the person they were adding to their system was able to meet their needs. Therefore, quality control was at the end of the line. After the system didn't work, they are very sorry.

We need to take a cue from the corporate world for our personal lives. The corporate arena says we are not going into victimization. You are going to verify if you are going to be a successful executive. "I'm sorry . . . I thought" means you were too lazy to verify and qualify your systems.

The next word is *qualify*. That means you ask, *"Is the system able to perform over a protracted period of time?"* Let's go back to buying a car. Say you kick the tires, drive the car down the street, and verify it can go seventy-five miles per hour. But what you didn't do was drive it for a long enough distance. So when you went to work the next day the car broke down on you. You found out later that the dealer put thick oil in the car that made it work well in the short term. You verified that the car could go seventy-five miles per hour, but you didn't qualify that it could work over a protracted period of time.

When you add people to your business system, ask yourself, *Are they going to hang in there over a protracted period of time?* For example, that key position you're training that new employee to fill has cost you a lot of time and training expense. Did you qualify that the employee will remain with you long enough to get the pay out on your investment?

In relationships, you really want to qualify that a person will perform over time. How many times do people put on a show for the person they are trying to "catch"? They can maintain the charade for a while, but in time the true character will come out. Qualifying deals specifically with performance over time. So check out their track record. Get to know the people in their environment. Find out what's in their potential. I want to know what your heart embraces as truth because you're going to act it out sooner or later.

When you qualify and verify, you look at people's pasts. But that doesn't negate the fact that in Christ we are new creatures. Old, bad files have passed away. So in that situation you need to look at the consistent NOW. If you used to be abusive, but you haven't been abusive for three years, great. But if at three years and one day you slip back into the old file, that's fair cause for concern.

Many people don't verify and qualify in romantic relationships because they aren't willing to turn down a person for their system who goes against the Word of God. In fact, in Bible times fathers and mothers would pick mates for their children because the parents wouldn't have to deal with the romantic emotions.

Once you get a hold of verifying and qualifying, you're going to do it to everything. Why suffer the consequences?

So, after I get to know my customer through research and development, design and redesign to meet customer changes, and test my systems through verifying and qualifying, I am ready to manufacture. First I design my standard operating procedure (SOP). I will give my written SOP to my quality control person, who will examine the materials before they go on line.

Step #4: Fish Boning. What should we do when the system falls outside acceptable ranges of variance? Profits are way down. The marriage has no passion. Your projects aren't getting done. We look at problems as so overwhelming, and we want to throw out the whole system.

If we verified and qualified that system in advance, we are not going to throw the whole system out. Instead we will find out which part went awry to throw a previously acceptable system out of range. Something unacceptable has entered into the system.

We no longer need to be victims when our systems fail.

We just need to *fish bone* the system. That means you look at the specific area that is out of order. You'll find your problem will exist in basically four quadrants: *people, material, equipment, and/or environment.*

Fish Boning

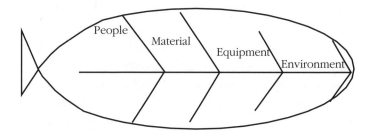

1. People. For example, you've got a nice kid, but he starts running around with a new group of kids when he changed schools. Now he has a real ugly attitude. Are you going to kick the kid out of the house? You could, but if you want to keep your relationship with the child, you do something else. You could change his friends and/or his school. Many of us would destroy the whole parenting system when all we needed was to repair one part of it.

2. Material. For example, you're feeling inadequate. You don't feel attractive. You have all these insecurities impacting your life. It could be that all you need to do is get another hairdo, and a hairdo could change your whole outlook on life. It could change you from one who felt totally depleted to one who is bold and self-confident. There are people who have missing teeth and won't talk in front of others. They think they are shy and something is wrong with them. There is nothing wrong with them other than their need to get their teeth fixed.

Again, we throw whole systems out without pinpointing the true problem. Maybe the relationship would have worked if you had taken that mate out for a date or bought her a dress. You could have saved the marriage. She had been saying all along, "I just want you to care about me. Show me some attention." Well, you didn't do that, so now instead of buying a one-hundred-dollar dress you've got a divorce that's costing you in the thousands. If you had invested wisely toward your customer you could have salvaged this relationship. But you didn't notice when the marriage started going outside acceptable ranges of variance.

3. Equipment. Here's a simple example. You have a good-paying job that you love, but you're angry with your manager because every morning you come to work five minutes late, and he gets in your face. You're five minutes late because your car is hard to start due to a bad battery. It only makes sense that if you want to keep your job, you will get a thirty-dollar battery to save a fifty-thousand-dollar-a-year job. You say, "I can't afford a battery," but then you get your hair and nails done or buy that new fishing set. Then when you get in trouble with your manager you say, "I'm a victim." You're not a victim. Get the right equipment.

4. Environment. For example, I know my child is a good kid, but I see him wearing gang clothing and starting to move in that arena. If I really want to save my child, what will I do? It might make sense for me to change my community, the environment he's growing up in. Maybe I can't afford to, but can I afford to lose a child?

Fish Boning in Eden

Adam and Eve were part of a perfect system in the Garden of Eden. God had verified and qualified that whenever He came they would fellowship with Him. But the day Adam and Eve ran from God, God recognized something was out of acceptable variance. He basically asked, "What has come into your mind (potential) and shaped your thinking (presuppositions)? You've been giving your attention to something else that has caused its spirit to come live in you. Who told you you were naked?" (See Genesis 3:10.)

God identified that Satan, the snake, had corrupted His system. God could have wiped out mankind right then. But instead He had in place the plan of redemption to fix the system so that man could be restored to fellowship with Him (acceptable variance).

Man was afraid of God because he recognized

the signs of being outside the acceptable range of variance. The Word of God says, "I did not give you the spirit of fear but of power and love and of a sound mind." (See 2 Timothy 1:7.) If you have a spirit of fear, someone has been changing and molding what belongs to God. You need to give your attention to God so that 1) His Spirit will live in you through His Word, and 2) your birthrights of confidence, courage, hope, belief, faith, and trust in God as the source of your hope will indwell you. Remember, what you give you attention to, its spirit will come to live in you. The devil comes to steal, kill, and destroy (John 10:10).

Throughput and Bottlenecks

We just talked about fish boning in order to solve whatever problem your system may be having. Now I want to look at a specific problem that often occurs. You have a system that is verified and qualified, but you can't produce product fast enough. In other words, you are working hard but not accomplishing all that needs to be done.

That is called a *throughput* problem. A throughput problem is generally caused by a bottleneck in your system. A bottleneck is an area of constraint.

I can go into one of my plants and quickly identify a bottleneck problem by whether there is backed up inventory on the assembly line. For example, there may be an imbalance of product flow. One product not flowing in balance through the assembly line can cause other products to be backed up. It's like a funnel. I can have all kinds of product in the open mouth of the funnel, but the output will be determined by the diameter of the spout. The spout's diameter is the bottleneck or area of constraint that governs the ability for product throughput.

Bottlenecks often occur when we try to release our potential. If you have a lot of potential but a low-capacity for hard work or discipline, you can be a genius and gifted, but you are not able to deliver it. You've been to school and got the degrees and the knowledge, but you have a bottleneck. You fear rejection or failure, so you don't start your career. Remember those voices from those past files? They may strain your capacity for risk taking and work potential. A lot of these bottlenecks come from negative programming early in your life.

In relationships you can recognize bottlenecks as backed up inventory, too. It is often unforgiveness. You told your mate, "I forgive you," but though he efforts to establish a clean, fresh relationship, you find you can't give him the loving throughput.

There may be people you really want to like in your family, but you have bad memories of what they did to you as a teenager or child. Now you don't even want to see them because you have a bottleneck of backed up inventory of unforgiveness.

A bottleneck of stinginess can manifest itself in your closet or garage. For example, is your closet stuffed with excess inventory of "I'll wear it some day" clothing? Holding on to things that are not needed and that bury you may indicate a lack of trust in God to supply your daily need. Some people are miserable because they have so much junk from the past that is crowding them out it makes them horrified to live in their own home environment, but they won't give it or throw it away. Their only answer is to build more closets to handle it.

People who are stuck in the past are often talking about what they used to be, what they were, but they are not giving you throughput now.

To fix our bottleneck problems, we need to go back into the files and reprogram those files. You need to apply what you learned in "Reprogram Your Subconscious Mind" and "Choose Who Pushes You." We did reprogramming by using repetition and not using the pronoun *it* so that you had to think before you spoke. Many of us have not practiced thinking. We've been slaves to conditioned negative habits of our pasts. In our spiritual lives, we start our systems with God as our customer, but bottlenecks come in and we stop giving God what He wants. In Revelation 3:14-16 God told the church at Laodicea, "You are lukewarm. You are not zealous." They had lost the passion for giving Him what He wanted. God said, "Since you are merely lukewarm, I will spit you out of my mouth!" (v. 16, TLB).

Improving a Good System

You've now read quite a bit about what to do when you have a problem in a system. Do you know what separates really successful people from those who merely do well? It's the willingness to look at a system that is working well and see how to make it work better.

Most of us only consider change when a system faces extinction. But change is most likely to succeed when it is done proactively (before the crisis).

How do you target areas for improvement? I start by making a list of things that aggravate me about a system. Then I identify the items on the list that are the greatest threat to the system's survival.

Before implementing a change, ask yourself the following questions. I've compiled this list with the help of Dr. Demings writings. You need to consider each question and give it an answer. No skipping!

- What is the cost?
- What's the method of change?
- What new people must come into our lives?
- What changes need to be made in equipment or materials around us that we use?
- What new skills will be required and for how many people?
- How will training come in these skills? (For example, all of our staff have books to read on updated management systems, and they must do book reports.)
- How will skills be used?
- How will we know if the customer is satisfied? (For example, I pass out forms to people who come to our Vertical Leap Seminars [see page i for information on how you can attend] and ask

127

them, "Are you satisfied? How can we improve?")

Here is a list of principles that guide me in making decisions. Any one of these principles can be life-changing for you, so I encourage you to read through the list slowly, making sure you comprehend each one.

- Create consistency of purpose for improvements and service to customer.
- Adapt a new philosophy where mistakes and negativism are unacceptable. Gather people around you who say, "You can do it."
- Manage by the 80-20 rule. We spend 80 percent of our time on people who only give us 20 percent of our production. They drain us. We should spend 80 percent of our time with the 20 percent who give us our 80 percent of production.
- Don't look to the masses for examples. Innovation is where we're going in the twenty-first century. If you're looking to the masses, you're looking to the past.
- Don't live by feelings alone.
- Improve consistently your service to the customer.
- Institute a training program.
- Institute a leadership program (mentoring).
- Drive out fear.
- Work as a team.
- Eliminate empty words and slogans.
- Don't set conditions on the process.

- Have pride in the quality of your teams' accomplishments because you share in one another's success.
- Education and retraining is a continual process.
- Take action to accomplish your goals.
- "OK" is not good enough to stay in business.
- Know what to do and then do it.
- Don't get nervous if a system starts varying. Recognize that variance is a part of any system and make sure it stays within your verified and qualified ranges.
- Know that planning requires predictions of how people and things will perform.
- Tests and experiences of the past can be helpful predictors, but they are not definitive.
- Tests and experiences are helpful, but we need to use all the knowledge around us.
- Know that systems and not individual skills determine how a process performs. Gravity is an example of a system. If you operate with respect to its laws, you can succeed. No matter how skilled you are, you cannot change gravity. If you work within a system you'll succeed, but if you insist on creating a new system, you're liable to waste time and hurt yourself.
- Know that only you can change your systems.

Review

If you really study what's in this chapter, you will

get more practical knowledge than many people get out of an entire year in business school.

It was a long chapter, so let's review what we've received. First you learned that a system is anything with one or more moving parts. Then you looked at how to operate a system successfully using statistical process control (SPC) to have quality control in the beginning of the line instead of at the end. Building a system according to SPC takes four steps: 1) research and development (Who are your customers, and what do they want?), 2) design and redesign (be innovative; be quick to change with the growth of your market), 3) testing (verify—is your system able to perform the task—and qualify—is your system able to perform over a protracted period of time?), and 4) fish boning (data drive the variances in people, material, equipment, and environment.)

We looked at bottleneck problems and how to solve them. Finally, when you have a system that works well, you can't stop working on it. The key to the future success is to improve on current success. I gave you the questions and principles you need to introduce innovation into a system.

Summary

Congratulations! You've read through all seven of the spiritual principles of success. I could end this book right here, but I feel there is one more necessary teaching to give you. Many people want to receive dreams, visions, ideas from God, but they don't know how to seek Him for them. The last chapter of this book will tell you how to do that.

APPLICATION QUESTIONS

1. SPC says to practice quality control at the beginning of the production line instead of at the end. How can you apply this principle to relationships? To business?

   _____

   _____

   _____

   _____

   _____

2. Think of an unproductive business or personal experience. In that situation, did you take the time to verify and qualify? What could you have done differently?

   _____

   _____

   _____

   _____

   _____

3. When you have a problem in a system, practice fish boning, which is identifying the specific area that is out of order and fixing it. Fish bone a problem in your life by looking at four quadrants—people, material, equipment, environment.

————————————————

————————————————

————————————————

————————————————

————————————————

4. Look back at the principles for decision making. Choose one and put it into practice today.

————————————————

————————————————

————————————————

————————————————

————————————————

Part 3

The Spiritual Dimension

Chapter 10

Seeking Spiritual Guidance

Now that you've read the seven spiritual principles, you need to ask yourself, *Have I received God's dream for me at this point in my life? Am I ahead of Him or behind Him or right in His timing?*

If you've got the vision and you're in the zone with God, then great! Stay connected to your Source, and be sure to keep reading this chapter because I'm going to give you the six steps to starting a business (or ministry!) with no money.

If God's dream for you is fuzzy right now, don't be discouraged. He knows what He wants you to do. He wouldn't have brought you this far if He didn't have a plan for you.

Right now I'm going to help you to go into your spiritual closet and talk to God about His plans for you. First of all, let me say that this is *not* transcendental meditation. This is going into your closet for prayer (Matt. 6:6) and shutting the door behind you so that you block out all distractions. Don't let your mind go empty. That's transcendental meditation (TM). Keep your mind stayed on Jesus, calling on His name, Jesus. He is your guide. He is your petitioned one. He is your Lord and Savior. Seek Him. He rewards those who diligently seek Him (Heb. 11:6).

I want to be very clear that you must seek God. There are many people who will meditate in order to contact a spirit guide or some inner power they believe lies within themselves. We are weak in ourselves, and we don't want to deal with satanic beings, so when meditating, we must focus on Jesus at all times.

One way you know a vision is of God is that it will be a desire of your heart (Heb. 8:10). David wrote, "Delight thyself also in the Lord; and he shall give thee the desires of thine heart" (Ps. 37:4, KJV). At the same time, a vision from God will never contradict His Word. God will not give you a vision to divorce your spouse and marry another. He will not lead you to lie, cheat, or steal. When you're hearing from God, you should feel an inner peace from the Holy Spirit. (See Colossians 3:15.) If you don't feel that peace, then refocus on Jesus and ask Him again to speak to you.

When you are ready to seek God, I want you to sit up straight in a chair. That's to keep you conscious. If your body is not disciplined, neither will your mind be. Now close your eyes and meditate on Jesus.

The Old Testament temple is our model for entering into God's presence. As you first approach Him, you are in the outer court, where your mind is busy with thoughts of where you could be and what you could be doing. You're going to have to break through the outer court.

Next is the inner court. Before you can enter here, you must go through a cleansing process.

When you come into God's presence and He requires you to change, you will have unrest in your spirit (Heb. 3:11). When you are off the path, it's in His presence that He will show you bottlenecks (areas of sin and selfishness) that He wants to eliminate so that He can download into you NOW. Since you have the blood of Jesus, you know how to repent and recommit to the Lord. (See 1 John 1:4–9.)

In the past you may have aborted a dream from God because you didn't trust Him. Now you can ask Him to impregnate you once again with your purpose.

The process of trusting God starts by determining if we are robbing Him. The Bible makes it very clear that if you aren't tithing and giving offerings that you are out of order and you haven't accomplished throughput. You have bottlenecks because you don't fully trust Him, and that's why your life has been hit and miss. You go to church, you do all of the right things, but there's no fruit because you don't trust Him. The key to kingdom economics is that you have to be sold out. When God is in full charge of our lives, we will be givers in all areas of life because He is a Giver. We will be dead to self and alive to Christ (Gal. 2:20).

Finally, you may enter the inner court. Time and space goes away in here. It's like being under anesthesia. To keep you from pain, the anesthesiologist gives you medication that keeps you balanced between life and death. In like manner, you want to balance between being awake and asleep.

You want to be comfortable while you're talking to God but not go to sleep. You have to discipline the flesh when it causes you to lose the battle. If you get sleepy, catch yourself, and don't give in. As you sit erect, hold your head up and face forward. Don't let your head fall to your chest. Your head falling is a good clue that sleep and the flesh are winning the battle. Be sure not to move a muscle. Stay focused on praising and worshipping Jesus.

Don't let it be OK to go unconscious when you go before God. That's what the enemy wants you to do. If you go unconscious you'll be pulling from old files, and you won't know the now. God wants you to be able to hear Him NOW. Remember, He is a NOW God. Remember, NOW has been defined as zero to five seconds of short-term conscious awareness before it moves to long-term memory.

When you are in that inner court, you may encounter the heavenly realm where your vision is already fulfilled. You are seeking to get in the zone with what God has already finished.

Get It in Detail

You may only understand your vision from God as a vague impression at first. But ultimately you must receive it in detail. Don't be afraid to seek the detail of the vision, because God knows it.

For example, Hattie and I had a dream to build the Alhatti Christian Resort. We had seen everything in the spirit realm, and then we went seeking it in the physical realm. Hattie had magazines and books all over the place on decorating, but she knew what she was looking for because she had already foreseen it in the spirit realm. She knew the right thing when it showed up.

You're going to have to be able to know the detail of what God is requiring of you. As an example, close your eyes right now. Can you remember how many pictures are on the wall in the room where you are sitting? How many plants? What knickknacks are on the shelves?

When God shows you His vision, He wants you to be so sensitive that you will see it in the utmost detail, just as Noah saw the ark and Moses saw the tabernacle (Heb. 8:5).

That's what I do before starting a production plant. I see the total project first in the spirit realm before I do it. I walk through the plant in my mind's eye. I look at the production lines and see how many people are working. I look at the equipment and make sure to see the name of the manufacturer of the equipment if possible. I look at the throughput, how fast product is coming off.

In summary, I take a detailed look at the people, equipment, material, and environment within the plant and office before I begin the process. Don't forget the paper clips and toilet paper, time clocks, pencils, telephones, trays, pictures for the walls, and so on. All of this is required to have an up and running facility, and somebody must foresee it to provide it.

When I bid a project, I am confident in our ability to perform as projected because I have seen the work in the spirit realm and have a plan for its execution. When a vision is of God, as you practice being in His presence, He will show you what to do in more and more detail.

Whether your vision is a factory, a dress shop, or a ministry, seek God for details in the same four areas we used for fish boning: people, material, equipment, and environment.

Consider each quadrant independently. Think about all the information an architect uses to decide where every joint must be placed in a building. In the same way, you must be the spiritual architect for God's vision given to you.

When God is doing a building project He will tell you how to do it exactly the way He wants it. When Moses built the tabernacle, God warned him to follow exactly the pattern of the heavenly tabernacle as shown to him (Heb. 8:5).

Be careful not to let other people "put their noses on His baby" because God won't be in it. When God has given you a vision, you have to spend more time getting confirmation from Him than you do from the world. Keep going back before the Lord to get the details. He wants His baby to look just like Him.

Six Steps to Starting a Business With No Money

Once you are pregnant with a detailed vision from God, then you are ready to birth it from the invisible to the visible. As any mother will tell you, a birth is one of the most painful and most satisfying experiences of life.

The six steps to starting a business that I am about to give you are completely unique. They are especially for Christians who want to be led by the Spirit of God in everything they do. Don't be deceived by their simplicity. They work.

Starting a Business Step #1: Don't doubt that God is God.

You are going to be doing things that are totally illogical. People won't understand, so you have to trust God. Worship is key to trusting God. Remember, worship is giving God praise and exaggerated respect. You are to focus your attention on Him.

Starting a Business Step #2: Don't limit God. Seek Him through dreams, visions, and ideas.

As you just learned, seek God in the inner court for His specific plan for you, and be sure to get the details! Keep going back to His presence again and again because He has an endless supply of creativity.

He is a rewarder of those who diligently seek Him (Heb. 11:6), so whatever you give your attention to, its spirit will come to live in you. You must be prepared to hear God's Word unto perception. Remember, *keechie keechie?* You can't do what you can't see.

Starting a Business Step #3: Don't compromise. Speak the vision.

You see people on television spending tons of money telling their visions. They know that some percentage of the people will buy into the vision. God will also have you tell your vision, but not just to anybody. He'll tell you where to go. God has people in place who have what you need and will help you. Jesus told His disciples exactly who to talk to about the colt. (See Mark 11:1–6.)

When your words are God's words they become light and cause changes in you and the people you meet. People will want to give you favor even though they've never met you before. They may wonder, "Why am I doing this? I don't know why I want to bless them so." God's Spirit spoke to them and said to give you favor.

There are times in my life when the Lord drops people into my spirit. I would see them walking down the street, and because we are a storehouse for Him, He would say, "Bless that person." I don't know them, and they don't know me, but I bless them.

The Lord told me to bless a woman who had just come out of a homeless shelter. I approached her, and she literally started running. She thought I was going to harm her even though she had probably just left this shelter with the prayer, "Oh, God, send someone to help me." But when the blessing came she started to run because her presuppositions may have been that prayer is a nice exercise, but people are out to hurt me. The end of the story is that we realized Hattie should approach her instead of me. So when Hattie came toward her, she stopped running, and we could bless her.

Don't let your presuppositions about other people keep God from blessing you through them.

Starting a Business Step #4: Write the vision.

I strongly urge you to use the appendix in the back of this book for writing out a business plan. It will help you in writing down details of the vision you will need.

God tells you what He wants, but you bring it into the second dimension by putting it onto paper. "Write the vision, and make it plain" (Hab. 2:2, KJV). It's hard. You have to think. This is the time for being a spiritual transcriber. God is the architect, however, you must bring it from the spirit realm to the physical realm through questions (who, what, when, where, why, and how). By putting these spiritual teeth to your vision, you can chew the biggest vision into digestible pieces one bite at a time.

Financial skill is as important in kingdom economics as it is in worldly economics. I have found a simple principle to be key.

Cash Flow Creating Wealth

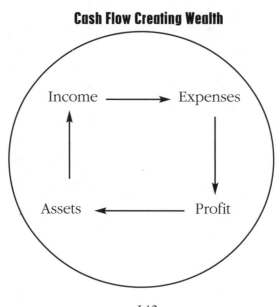

Invest in Assets, Not Liabilities. The body of Christ has been appointed to be the head not the tail (Deut. 28:13), the lenders and not the borrowers. That means we need to understand *cash flow,* not just in the financial sense but in the spiritual sense as well. Poverty is often a result of investing our resources/talents poorly. If we invest in assets, they should grow to create more income. A cash flow to wealth results from the principle of turning assets to income minus expenses equalling profit reinvested in assets. This cycle continues until wealth goals are achieved.

A cash flow to poverty results from turning assets to income minus expenses equalling profit/loss reinvested in debt, which becomes a liability.

Cash Flow Creating Poverty

Note the movement of assets to debt and liability that perpetuates the poverty cycle. We are conditioned by advertisement and commercials to invest in our lusts and not our need. Excess vanity purchases place our assets in things that will not produce a profit.

For example, people buy a car and go into debt. They think they are creating an asset but they may really be creating a liability. For example, they pay more for the car than what they can sell it for. They invest a lot of money into maintaining the car, going into debt trying to keep up the property. That debt becomes a liability. Let's say they borrow money to repair the car. They have to pay it off, further increasing their expenses. The value of their car is not increasing at the rate of their expenses.

Matthew 25:14–30 tells us of three men who were given assets to invest for profit on behalf of their master. Two invested wisely and doubled their assets. When their master returned, they gave to him their gained profits. The third man put his talent into the ground, and Scripture tells us that the master was very angry, calling him lazy and slothful. He was challenged as to why he had buried his talent rather than put the talent to work in a bank creating cash flow through usury (interest).

This Scripture further informs us that what little this man had was taken from him and given to the man that had acquired the greatest return. "For the man who uses well what he is given shall be given more, and he shall have abundance. But from the man who is unfaithful, even what little responsibility he has shall be taken from him" (Matt. 25:29, TLB).

Daily we make decisions about where to invest our assets. Are they put in things that produce life or death? Deuteronomy 28 tells us that God's words are assets that will make us prosperous if we will hear them and do them. What words do we speak to our marriages, our children, ourselves? Are they words that will bring profit and become assets in our lives and the lives of others? Or are they words of cursing that will result in a poverty spirit? God has invested His assets (His Word) into us that we may produce profits.

Starting a Business Step #5: Don't sit—move!

Time management is crucial to any system. Here's a good way to decide what to spend time on. Learn to identify tasks according to whether or not they are important and whether or not they are critical (need to be done right away).

Time Management Matrix

	Critical	Not Critical
Important	Important/ Critical 10%	Important/ Not critical 87%
Not Important	Not important/ Critical 3%	Not important/ Not critical 0%

Eighty-seven percent of your time should be

given to important and not critical work. This is doing problem solving before the problems become emergencies.

Ten percent of time should be spent on the important and critical. There will always be emergencies that crop up outside of our control. However, if we spend most of our time in the important and not critical sector, we should be able to reduce the time in important and critical sector.

Three percent of time will be spent in the not important but critical sector. This quadrant deals with issues that are critical to other people's systems but not important to your system. Administrate to others as much of this sector's work as possible. You must be very careful that your important and not critical time is not taken up by the crises caused by others' poor planning.

You should endeavor to spend zero percent— no time at all—in the not important and not critical sector. Activities in this sector are the time wasters, such as idle phone calls and television browsing. This sector brings no value to your system.

As you move toward the vision, God will intervene on your behalf in three ways:

1. He shows or tells you how to make it.
2. He draws a blessing to you.
3. He tells you where to go get it.

It's not by power or by might, but it's by His Spirit (Ezek. 4:6). As you keep your mind stayed on Him through worship and praise, His Spirit will be quickened in you, and He will show you where to go and you will know what to say.

Remember, Pray in faith • Say (-Doubt+Belief) Forgiveness=Things. Your attitude must be one of believing God, and this attitude of godly confidence and courage will take you into places where others may fear to tread or have failed. However, you will not fail. You are in the zone. You have bonded with God and will have His favor upon you. So go/move. He will be with you.

Starting a Business Step #6: Don't quit. Persist until you succeed.

What if the vision doesn't come into reality? You keep working. How long do you work? Until it happens. Don't quit. You must be willing to fail often to succeed only once. Persistence requires:

- a definiteness of purpose backed by a burning desire for its fulfillment
- a definite plan
- a positive mind closed against negative influences
- a relationship with people who will encourage you to follow through with your plans and purpose
- accurate knowledge
- resistance to fear of criticism

You're dealing with two realities. Worldly and kingdom. You will go through challenges as you move in obedience. A good example is the testimony of best-selling author Bishop T. D. Jakes. People say his success was overnight. Bishop Jakes says he has been teaching for years. Now is just God's time for favor. He isn't doing anything different than he had been doing.

That's the key to kingdom economics. It's not by power or might. It's by God's favor. As you obey God, He in His time will do it. But that doesn't mean you stop working.

Do you see the unique spiritual dimension of the six steps to starting a business with no money? Yes, for your business you'll also need loans, property, employees, and many other practical things. That's why I'm giving you a business plan and business documents in the appendices. But remember that if you major on the majors, the minors will take care of themselves. Major on the spiritual things, and the physical things will be drawn unto you. (See Deuteronomy 28:1–14.)

Will You Practice What You Learned?

In the beginning of this book I asked you write down a dream from God that is struggling for life. Go back and look at what you wrote down (or pray again about what God's vision for you may be.)

Are you going to end up saying "I'm sorry" about this dream? Or are you going take the Vertical Leap and be moved to succeed from the inside rather than accept failure from the outside. I believe you are ready to succeed.

Remember the two conditions upon which all of our spiritual principles rest: 1) Stay conscious, and 2) Do it NOW. Do not fall back into your old habits. Use your consciousness to make good decisions. Don't wait until you are ready to move. When God says move, do it NOW!

Practice the seven spiritual principles:

1. See It on the Inside
2. Bond With Your Source
3. Make the Invisible Visible
4. Create; Don't Just Trade
5. Reprogram Your Subconscious Mind
6. Choose Who Pushes You
7. Analyze Your System

When you need answers, go into the inner court of prayer and seek God's guidance. (See Matthew 7:7.)

God has an awesome mission for your life that only you can fulfill. He has programmed it into your DNA, and when you are following that vision, you are going to change the world for the better. Thank you in advance for birthing your dream!

APPLICATION QUESTIONS

1. Effort to enter into the inner court of God's presence. If God brings to your mind areas of tightness or selfishness, write down how you could resolve them.

_____

_____

_____

_____

2. Has God given you a general impression of a dream, vision, or idea? Write it down.

_____

_____

_____

_____

3. Has God given you any details about the dream, vision, or idea? Write them down.

_____

_____

_____

_____

4. Which of the seven spiritual principles of success do you think would help you the most right now? Go back and reread that chapter.

_____

_____

_____

_____

Appendix A

The Business Plan

The purpose of a business plan is to help you see the vision exactly by writing it down (Hab 2:2). You are asked questions that lead you to answers that lead you to choices. It starts with your ability to think NOW.

Go through the business plan when you are in the inner court with God. He'll answer questions for you. It'll be revelation. When you have a hard time answering a question, spend time with Him until you have the peace.

The answers God gives you will not be the answers He gives me. He may want you to do something He told me not to do. We are to pray one for another and not judge. Peter wanted Jesus to tell him what John was to do. The Lord said, "Don't you worry about what I tell him. You just do what I tell you to do." (See John 21:20–22.)

God will also send you to people who can help answer questions or send you out to do research through books and magazines.

The plan I'm offering here is flexible, but it isn't the all-in-all business plan. You may need a business plan that is specific to your industry, and you can find it at a library or on the internet.

You won't necessarily answer these questions in order. You may have to come back to various points as you research. *Remember, God does not lead you through answers. He leads you through questions. On the other side of a question is an answer.* The Word of God says we have not because we ask not (James 4:3). It also states in Matthew 7:7, "Ask, and it shall be given you . . ." The business plan is the framework you will use to birth your vision. Many of the questions you will need to birth your vision from the spiritual realm of ideas to the physical realm of a physical plan are set before you. Remember, God is the Father of your vision, and you are His bride. He wants His babies to look just like Him, so only you can do the grunt work of birthing them.

Business Plan Worksheets

☐ Heading for Business Loan Request

☐ Cover Letter for Business Loan

☐ Loan Contacts

☐ Statement of Purpose

☐ Business Description

☐ Market Analysis

☐ Competition Analysis

☐ Location Analysis

☐ Management

☐ Personnel

☐ Financial Information

Note: *Many of the questions in the worksheets require detailed answers. Use a computer or additional paper for your responses.*

Worksheet I:
Heading for Business Loan Request

Business name _____

Business
location address _____

Business
mailing address _____

Business
telephone number _____

Tax identification number _____

List the principals in your company:

Name _____

Business title _____

Home address _____

Telephone number _____

Social security number _____

Name _____

Business title _____

Home address _____

Telephone number _____

Social security number _____

Appendix A: The Business Plan

Name _____

Business title _____

Home address _____

Telephone number _____

Social security number _____

Name _____

Business title _____

Home address _____

Telephone number _____

Social security number _____

Worksheet 2:
Cover Letter for Business Loan

Be sure to use your letterhead. At the top of the letter use the heading that you prepared from Worksheet 1. This cover letter includes the six subjects that must be covered. You may expand it, but it should not be more than one page.

Gentlemen:

I/We/am/are requesting a loan in the amount of $_____ for the purpose of _____. I/We/would like the repayment over _____ years.

The source of repayment is from _____.

Our secondary source of repayment is _____. _____ is offered as collateral, having an approximate equity value of $ _____.

If you have any questions concerning this request or the business plan, please contact me at _____. Thank you for your consideration.

Sincerely,

Worksheet 3:
Loan Contacts

Contact person
at lending agency _____
Telephone number _____

Accountant _____
Firm _____
Address _____
Telephone number _____

Attorney _____
Firm _____
Address _____
Telephone number _____

Banker _____
Bank name _____
Address _____
Telephone number _____

Business consultant _____
Firm _____
Address _____
Telephone number _____

Insurance agent _____
Insurance company _____
Address _____
Telephone number _____

Worksheet 4:
Statement of Purpose

1. Describe the purpose and goals of your business.
2. Why do you or did you take over or start this business?
3. What experience and credentials do you have to manage this business?
4. How much money will you need and where will you get it?

Borrowed	$	_____
Your investment	$	_____
Other's investments	$	_____
TOTAL	$	_____

5. How will the funds be used?
6. How will the money benefit the business?
7. Why does this loan/investment make sense?
8. What are the terms of repayment for the loan? (Answer in more detail than in the cover letter.)
9. What is the repayment source? (Answer in detail.)
10. What collateral are you offering, and what is its current market value? (Answer in detail.)
11. Who owns the collateral, and if not you, will they pledge it?

Worksheet 5:
Business Description

1. What is the legal description of your business (proprietorship, partnership, or corporation)?

2. If your business is a corporation, in which state have you incorporated?

3. For tax purposes, is the corporation subchapter S or standard?

4. What type of business is this (retail, wholesale, service, or manufacturing)?

5. What is the status of your business (new, start up, ongoing expansion, or takeover existing)?

6. Date your business started or will start?

7. If your business is existing, attach a history since inception.

8. What schedule will your business keep? What months, days, and hours is (will) your business be open and operational?

9. If your business is seasonal, detail how you will adjust your time schedule, inventory, and personnel.

10. Who are your suppliers and what will they be supplying to your business?

11. What are your suppliers' terms, and is trade credit available?

12. Have you contacted your suppliers for quotes? What are they?

13. Have you requested managerial and/or technical assistance from your suppliers?

14. Who are the people to whom you were directed for assistance?

15. If the work you do is contracted, include the terms, contracts, letters of intent, and referrals from past jobs. Attach.

16. If you are contracting work out for your product or service, who is/are the contractors and what are the terms? Attach a copy of the terms.

Worksheet 6:
Market Analysis

1. Who is your target market (neighborhood, socioeconomic, ethnic, age, sex)?
2. How would you describe the size of your market?
3. What percent of the market will you capture and why?
4. Does your market have growth potential? Why?
5. As the market increases, does your percent share increase or decrease? Why?
6. If you have plans, specifications, or artist renderings for work to be done, whether it be for your customer or yourself, include them.
7. What is special about this business?
8. Why will your business be profitable?
9. Have you researched this business? What are the results?
10. How will you meet the demand of your market?
11. Will increased sales cause a drain on the working capital you have? How will you overcome this?
12. How do you arrive at a price for your service, product, or merchandise? Will you make a fair profit with your price? Will your price remain competitive? Quote comparisons.
13. How are you going to market your service or product?

14. What advertising media will you use and what is the cost?
15. Why are you going to use that media?
16. What is your advertising budget and time schedule?
17. Who will help you with your advertising?
18. Are you going to change your mix of service or products?
19. Why can you service your market better than your competition?
20. Will you offer your customers credit? How?
21. How will you handle paying customers?
22. Are you going to accept credit cards? Which ones?
23. Attach logos brochures, ads, menus, and so on.

Worksheet 7:
Competition Analysis

1. Who are your nearest competitors? List at least six.

2. What will make you better than they are?

3. How is their business doing? Up? Down? Why?

4. How are you similar to them? How are you different?

5. Where are they strong? Weak?

6. What have you learned from watching them?

7. What is their percent of your market?

8. How will you get more of that market?

9. Comments about your competition.

Worksheet 8:
Location Analysis

1. Why have you chosen this location?

2. Give a general description of your neighborhood.

3. What are the zoning laws?

4. What other businesses are in the area?

5. Have you considered other areas? Which areas? Why?

6. Why is this location the best choice for your business?

7. What affect does this location have on your costs?

Worksheet 9:
Management

1. Attach resumes of the principals and key personnel.

2. What related work experience do they have?

3. What are the duties and responsibilities of each principal and key employee? Include job descriptions.

4. List starting salary, salary range, and fringe benefits for each position.

5. What management resources are available from outside sources, and where are they located?

6. Are you prepared to anticipate changes in location? How?

7. Why is this the right building for your business?

8. Is your building leased or owned by you?

9. If you have a lease, what are the terms, conditions, length, and cost? (Include copy of lease.)

10. What renovations are needed, if any? Describe them. (Get quotes from multiple contracts and include.)

Worksheet 10:
Personnel

1. What are your present and future personnel needs?

2. How available are employees? Where will you find them?

3. What skills must your employees have?

4. What training do your employees need, and how will you accomplish this?

5. Do you need full-time or part-time help? (Include a schedule of work hours.)

6. Are you going to allow overtime?

7. How much are you going to pay each position? Hourly? Weekly?

8. What fringe benefits are you going to offer your employees, and what will those benefits cost?

Worksheet II:
Financial Information

1. Supply last three years of balance sheets (or opening balance sheet for a new business). See below for an explanation of balance sheets.
2. Supply last three years of operating statements. See below for an explanation of profit and loss statements.
3. Supply projected operating statements, projected income statements, and projected balance sheets for the first year by month, second year by quarter, and third year by year.
4. Supply projected cash flow for the first year by month. See below for an explanation of cash flow.
5. Supply a break even analysis.
6. Supply a capital equipment list with serial numbers, cost, or value.
7. Supply appraisals of real estate, equipment, vehicles, and machinery.
8. Supply current personal financial statements for each borrower, principal, guarantor, co-signer, or endorser.
9. Supply any other pertinent financial information that would be helpful, for example, personal or business tax returns, contracts, letters of intent to do business.

Balance Sheets. The formula is:

**Assets - Liabilities = Net Worth
(or Owner's Equity)**

Assets are what you claim to own. Liabilities are what you owe against what you claim to own. For example, you claim to own a car valued at twenty thousand dollars, however, your note to the bank on that car is twelve thousand dollars. Your net worth (owner's equity), therefore, is eight thousand dollars. The way you make your balance sheet balance is by adding your owner's equity plus your total liability, and they should equal your total assets. I could have a multimillion-dollar business and still be doing poorly if my liabilities exceed my assets. It happens all the time. It's not how big you are. It's about making sure your assets are greater than your liabilities.

Profit and Loss (P & L). Most people think there is a standard form for doing a profit and loss statement. There isn't. It's driven by the business and the information you want revealed to you so you can manage your business. I am very particular about wanting to know my business expenses in detail where others may want to know them generally. The principle for calculating profit and loss is as follows:

Income is the capital you have coming in from your customers. Expenses are the costs incurred to create the product that you sold to the customer creating capital. The difference is your profit or loss. For example, you sell ice cream for a dollar a cone. It costs you twenty five cents for the cone and the ice cream, fifty cents for your labor, ice cream stand, advertisement and so on; therefore expenses total seventy five cents. That leaves you with a profit of twenty five cents per cone.

Sample Profit and Loss Statement for Ice Cream Business

Income	1.00
minus expenses	<u>−.75</u>
equals profit	+.25

(This example is quite simplistic. You really need to look at this on a monthly basis and projection over twelve months.)

Cash Flow. Cash flow is based on the same principle as profit and loss except that one's profit/loss for the month is flowed over to the following month's income stream. So the formula is income minus expenses equals profit or loss, which is then flowed over into the next month's income stream. Cash flow is a very important document to an entrepreneur because it gives him the ability to project future cash accumulation, which can be used for purchasing or repayment of debt.

Investors and vendors will want to see your cash flow projections. What if you show them a profit and loss statement where at the end of the month the expenses are greater than the income? If it doesn't look like it's going to change, the investors and vendors won't want to work with you.

Often people spend more than they bring in. That's why they go bankrupt. They are doomed to failure. There are multibillion-dollar businesses that fail because they don't control their expenses. No matter how big you are, if your expenses are greater than your income, eventually you will fail.

All of these are very simplistic explanations, but these principles can be based on individual preferences. I could go into more detail, but that would be better for another book.

Appendix B

Test Your Knowledge

1. What is redemption? *Something in place, taken out of place, and put back into its proper place.*
2. How long is NOW? *Zero to five seconds.*
3. What are the characteristics of principles? *Principles are applicable to all areas of life. Principles are spiritual and do not change. Facts are based on conditions that are subject to change. Principles create facts.*
4. What is the meaning of the keechie keechie teaching? *You can't believe what you can't see.*
5. What will happen when we are bonded to God? *He downloads a vision into us. We will have passion, which leads to actions, which lead to things, then habits, then character, which forms a destiny, which crystallizes into circumstances.*

5. What are the three ways God intervenes on our behalf?

- *He shows or tells you how to make it.*
- *He draws a blessing to you.*
- *He tells you where to go get it.*

6. What are your birthrights? *Confidence, courage, hope, belief, faith, and trust in the source of your hope.*
7. What is balancing? *Letting the lesser things die that the greater may live*
8. What is discipline? *Delaying gratification.*
9. How do you change a bad habit? *You replace it with a good habit.*
10. How do you form a good habit? *REPOH.* Repetition *makes it easy,* easy *makes it a pleasure,* pleasure *makes you do it* often, *doing it often makes a* habit.
11. What are three ways to reprogram an old file in your subconscious mind? *Repetition, shock, and God's divine plan (worship and prayer).*
12. What are the four ways the brain acquires information? *Five senses, reasoning, intuition, culture/authority.*
13. What are the four functions of the conscious mind? *Recognize, identify, organize, and file.*
14. What are the three steps for changing hope into a material thing? (hope to a thing teaching) *You start with hope that comes from God. You make a decision to go from hope to belief. Then you take*

action to go from belief to faith. Finally, you practice patience to go from having faith to having the material thing. The power to move from step to step comes from touchstoning, which is remembering God's goodness and praising Him, which builds trust in God, the source of your hope.

15. Write Mark 11:22-25 as an algebraic formula.

Pf • S(-D+B)Fg = Things
Pray in faith • Say(-Doubt + Belief)Forgiveness = Things

16. What is the definition of commerce? *Reaching outside of one's own self or borders in order to be complete.*
17. What are the three types of commerce? *War, barter and trade, and creativity.*
18. What are the differences between God's predestined timeline and man's logical timeline? *God sees time from the end to the beginning (right to left) while man sees it from beginning to end (left to right).*
19. What does it mean to say out of the greater flows the lesser? *The higher dimensions contain the lower dimensions.*
20. Name the six steps for starting a business with no money.

- *Don't doubt that God is God.*
- *Don't limit God. Seek Him through dreams, visions, and ideas.*

- *Don't compromise. Speak the vision.*
- *Write the vision.*
- *Don't sit—move!*
- *Don't quit—persist until you succeed.*
- *How do you know you're called of God?*
- *Driven out of your comfort zone.*
- *Rendered helpless/dependent on others.*
- *Dark time of the soul—misunderstood.*

21. Does God lead by questions or by answers? *Questions.*
22. Break down the meaning of the word because. Be *is "to exist" and* cause *is "to incite to action."*
23. What is the corridor principle? *As a man moves he draws unto himself the desires of his heart.*
24. What is the scriptural foundation for the corridor principle? *Matthew 6:33: "Seek ye first the kingdom of God, and his righteousness; and all these things shall be added unto you (KJV).*

Appendix C

How to Know You Are a Child of God

You cannot be fulfilled on the outside until you have been fulfilled on the inside. This can only happen when you receive Jesus into your heart. If you have a longing in your heart for God, say this prayer with me now:

Lord Jesus, I invite You into my heart. I know that I have sinned and failed to do what is right in Your sight. I ask You to forgive me. Come into my heart. Be my Lord (Boss) and Savior (Protector) that I may live for You. In Jesus' name, amen.

If you prayed that prayer, and you have confessed with your mouth and believed in your heart that Jesus Christ is Lord and that He died on the cross and rose from the grave to save you from sin, the Bible assures you that you are saved. The Bible will tell you all the wonderful things that come with making this decision. (See Romans 10:9–10.) Let me tell you a little bit about what it means.

You have made a Vertical Leap into the family of God. Jesus came into your heart by His Holy Spirit, and He forgave you for the wrong things you have done. (See Revelation. 3:20.) You passed out of death and into life (John 5:24). God has given you eternal life in His Son Jesus (1 John 5:11). You have been born again and are a new creation (2 Cor. 5:17). It is no longer you that lives, but Christ living in you (Gal. 2:20). You are a child of the King (Rom. 8:16).

Congratulations!

Meet the Hollingsworths

Al and Hattie Hollingsworth are successful entrepreneurs, whose heart is to help others succeed with the visions, dreams, and ideas God gives to them.

They founded and operate a multimillion-dollar contract packaging business called Aldelano Corporation, whose clients include Kellogg's, Proctor and Gamble, and General Mills. Aldelano provides packaging for cereals, cake mixes, potato chips and many other products that are sold in club stores such as Sam's Wholesale, Cosco and the Price Club. The company has major plants and offices in Michigan, Ohio, Tennessee, and California.

Due to his business skill, Al Hollingsworth was honored as the National Minority Businessman of the Year by the U.S. Department of Commerce and received the Black Entrepreneur Award from the National Association of Market Developers.

Operating a successful business, however, is

only one of the Hollingsworth's endeavors. While serving as economic development commissioner for the state of California, they recognized that urban youth would soon face an economic crisis and wanted to give them an alternative to gangs, drugs, and hopelessness. Al and Hattie created a business training program for youth that has trained thousands of young people in the United States and Africa. Several trainings have also been in Japan and Switzerland. The Youth for Business B.O.S.S. program has certified trainers throughout the country who are currently operating programs. (B.O.S.S. stands for "Building On Spiritual Substance.")

Because of demand from the parents of youth in the program, they went on to form Christian Business Ministries, which offers training for adults. Upon completion of Vertical Leap training, adults are encouraged to partner with B.O.S.S. the Movement to train youth in the mission field of their own communities. Many sponsor Vertical Leap Seminars in their own cities.

To support the ministry, the Hollingsworths purchased 121 acres in the San Jacinto Mountains above Palm Springs, California, where they have developed the Alhatti Christian Resort as a conference center. The grounds are dedicated to the advancement of the gospel of Jesus Christ and are available for use by churches, businesses, and organizations in agreement with that goal. Vertical Leap Seminars are conducted there regularly.

The Hollingsworths enjoy a happy marriage and are the proud parents of three children and grandparents of five.

Founded by Al and Hattie Hollingsworth, the vision of Christian Business Ministries is to make a positive impact for the kingdom of God by ministering Christian business and leadership principles to adults and youth throughout the world. CBM's primary mission is to be instrumental in winning back America for Jesus by teaching the relevance of God and His Word in meeting each one's need for success in every area of one's life. CBM's outreach to youth is called B.O.S.S. the Movement.

B.O.S.S. the Movement

B.O.S.S. the Movement is based on the belief that youth have creative potentials that can richly provide them with the resources to be successful in the twenty-first century. These potentials can be unleashed with the right attention, training, and learning environment, all centered around Jesus Christ and His Word. The goal of B.O.S.S. training is to develop well-groomed, professional, spiritual confident and highly trained people who will establish viable economic systems extending far beyond the boundaries of their immediate living environments. The curriculum is designed for youth ages seven to seventeen—particularly those living in urban poverty—but it can be used successfully with youth of any background.

For more information, call:

1-888-559-BOSS
or
909-861-3846
or visit the web site at
www.bossthemovement.com

CHRISTIAN RESORT

It is unmistakable—the hush, the calm, the peace of God that abides at the Alhatti Christian Resort. Cradled in the tall whispering pines of the San Jacinto Mountains above Palm Springs, the resort built by Al and Hattie Hollingsworth is the ideal location for a retreat, leadership meeting, family reunion, youth camp, wedding, anniversary, honeymoon, prayer retreat, personal renewal, or vacation. The luxurious facilities include:

Cottages

Built with simple elegance in mind, cottages have down comforters, cassette tape players, fireplaces (in most) and many upgraded amenities.

Women's Dorm

Bouquets and bows is the theme of the ladies suite, which offers a bright, cheerful place for women to commune together. Down comforters and personal lockers are included.

Men's Dorm

A wood burning stove and richly paneled walls create a masculine atmosphere where Christian brothers can fellowship and grow together in Christ.

Chapel Hill

Situated with a spectacular sunset view of Hemet Valley, Chapel Hill provides an ideal setting for fellowship with God. It's an ideal place for worship services or weddings.

The Amphitheater

Canopied by towering pines and surrounded by a bubbling brook and waterfalls, this outdoor meeting area provides another excellent venue for group activities or personal quiet time with the Lord.

Lake

A one-acre lake stocked with trout, bluegill, and catfish, along with a multitude of nature's most beautiful birds, provides a unique and peaceful atmosphere for relaxation or fishing.

Sports Courts

Outdoor activities abound for the athletically inspired. Enjoy a game of tennis, volleyball, basketball, or chip n' putt golf and then unwind in the jacuzzi.

Walking Trails

The testimony of God's magnificent hand is appreciated most on our walking trails nestled among the pines by natural creeks and a waterfall.

The Alhatti Christian Resort

23551 Highway 243
P.O. Box 597
Idyllwild, CA 92549
Phone: 909-659-2066
Fax: 909-659-4636
Web site: www.alhatti.com

Products Available

Vertical Leap (book)

Vertical Leap Jerseys
(available in black and yellow,
white and black, red and black)

Vertical Leap Baseball Caps
(available in yellow, red or white on black)

A wide variety of audio tapes

For more information, contact:

Christian Business Ministries

B.O.S.S. the Movement
P.O. Box 5516
Diamond Bar, CA 91765-5516

1-888-559-BOSS
909-861-3846
Fax: 909-861-6039
Web site: www.bossthemovement.com